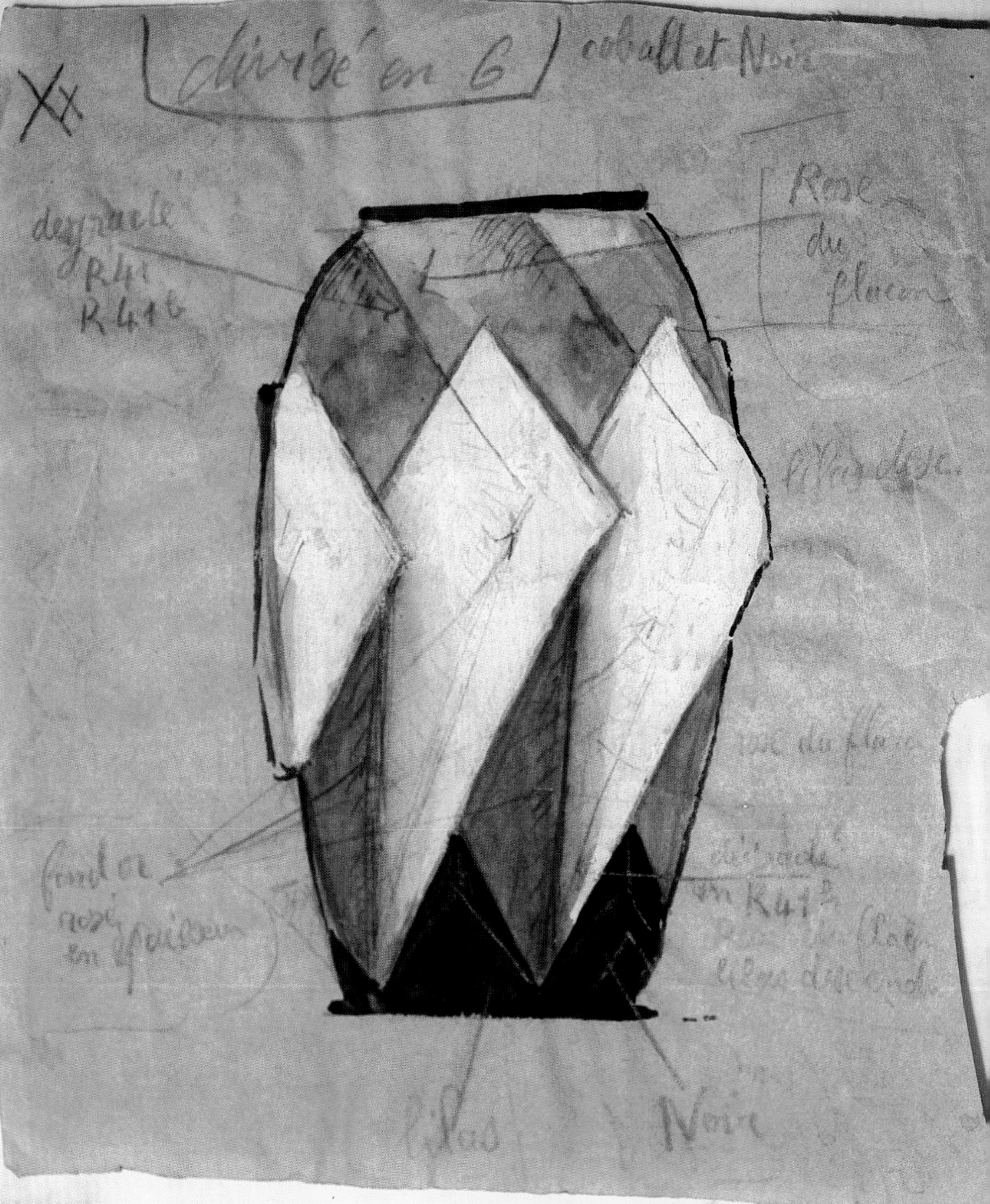

XX

(divisé en 6) cobalt et Noir

dégradé
R41
R416

Rose
du
flacon

fond or
rosé
en épaisseur

rose du flacon

dégradé
en R41?
flacon
lilas dégradé

lilas   Noir

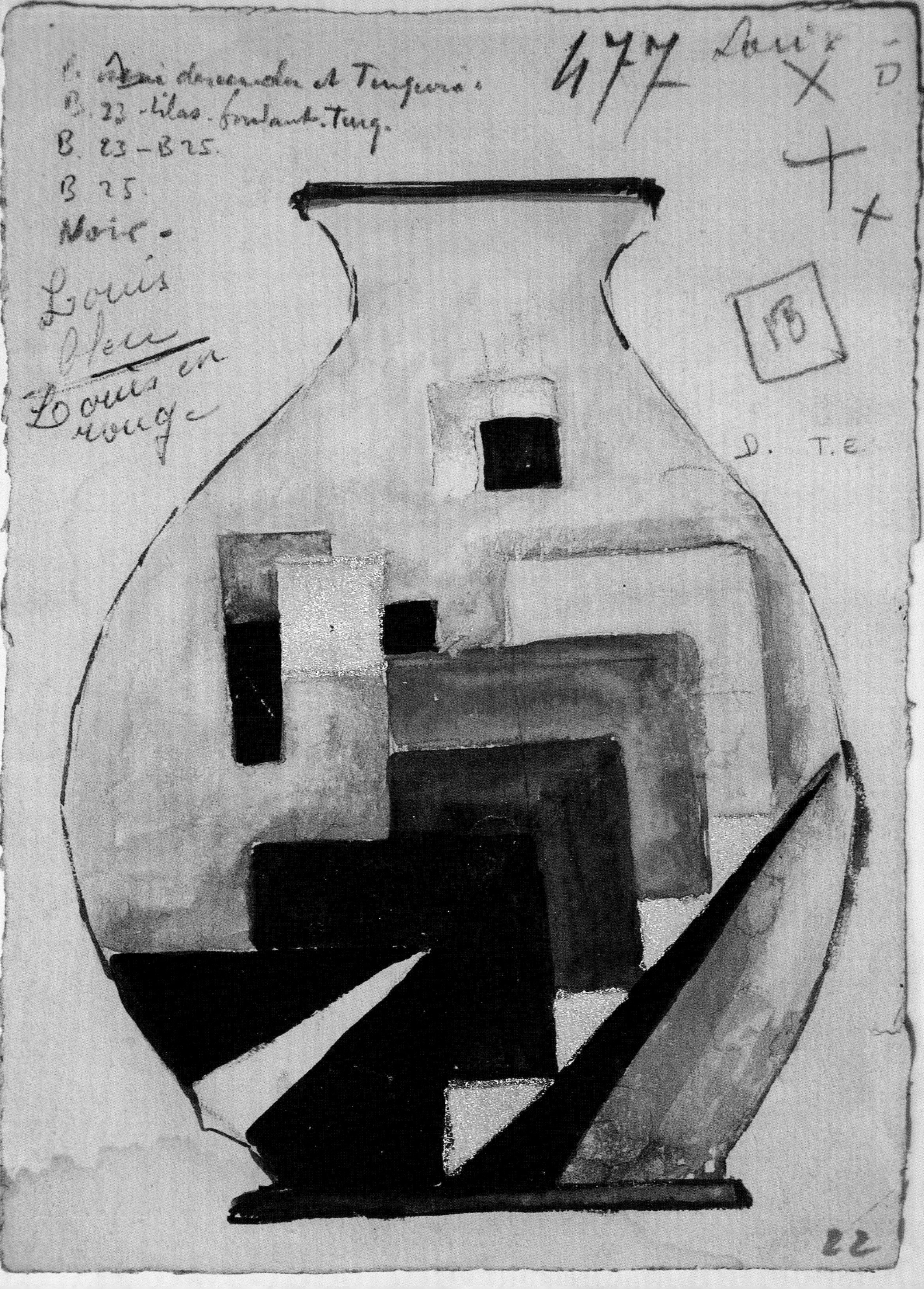
477
B. 23 - B 25.
B 25.
Noir -
Louis
Louis en rouge
D. T.E
22

Camille Fauré:
Impossible Objects

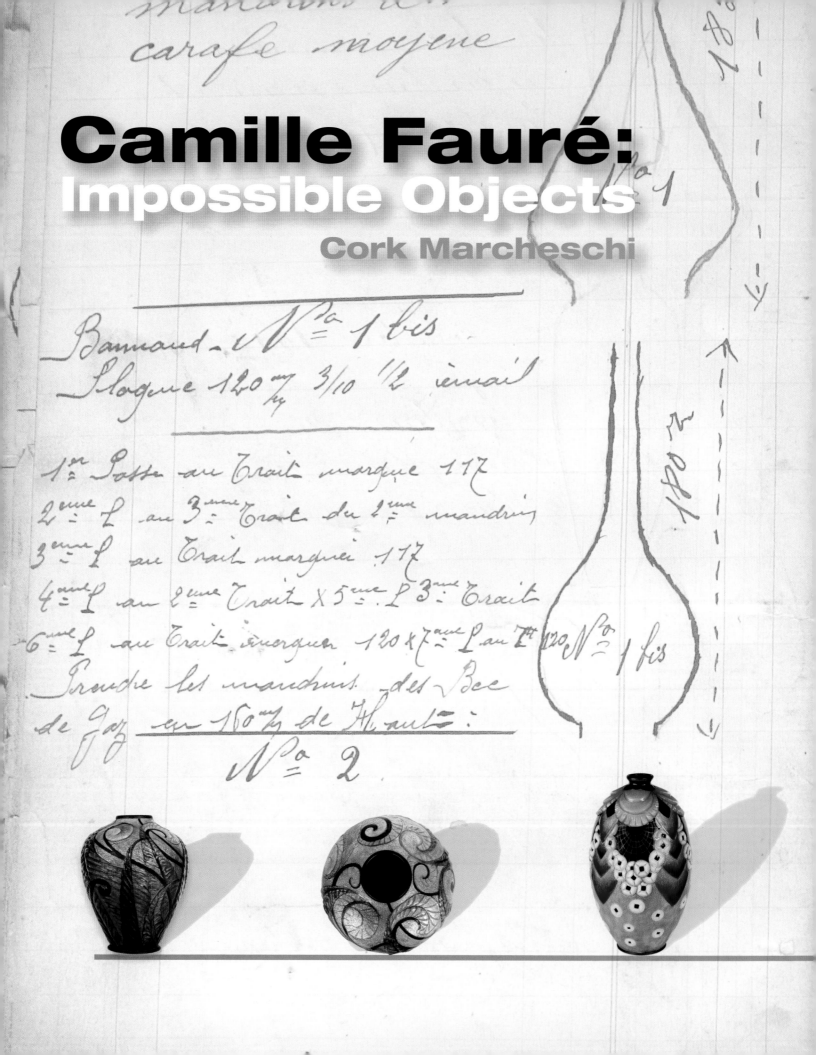

Camille Fauré:
Impossible Objects
Cork Marcheschi

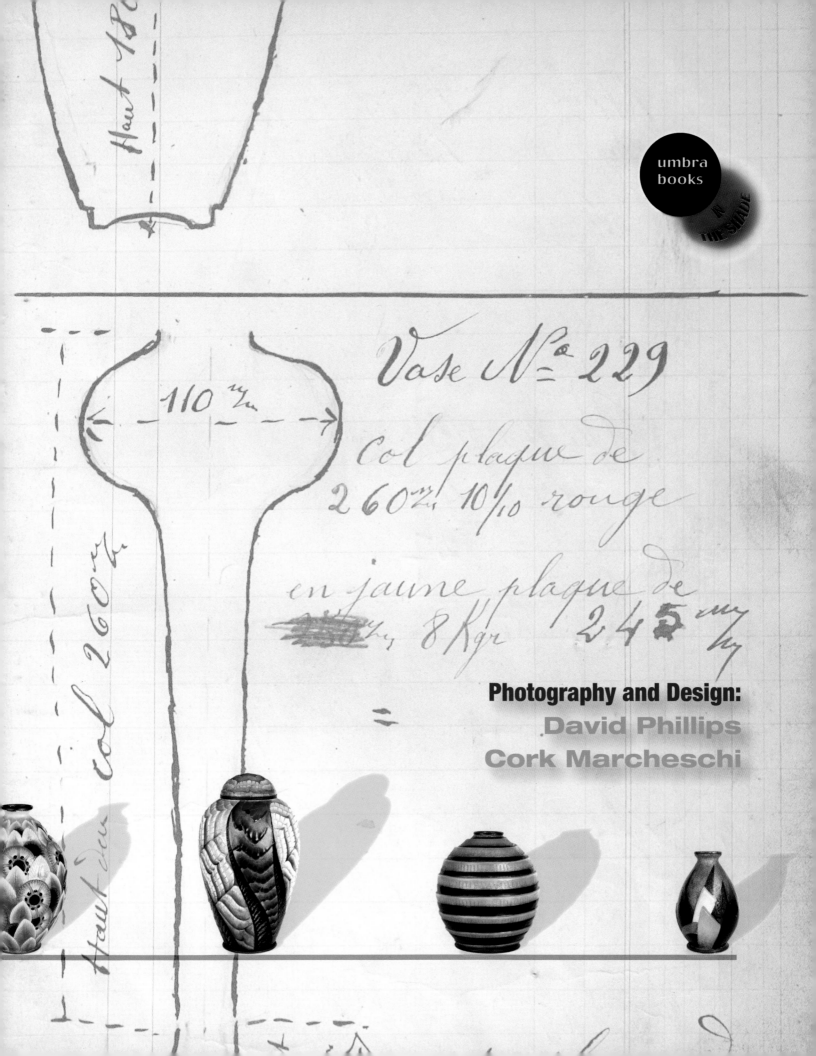

umbra
books

IN THE SHADE

Vase Nᵒ 229

col plaque de

260ᵐ 10/10 rouge

en jaune plaque de

8 Kgr 245ᵐᵐ/kg

Photography and Design:
David Phillips
Cork Marcheschi

Designed and typeset by David Phillips.
Main photographer: David Phillips

Printed in China.

Library of Congress
Cataloging-in-Publication Data
Marcheschi, Cork
Camille Fauré: Impossible Objects/Cork
Marcheschi
ISBN0-615-13229-4

CORK MARCHESCHI is a San Fran-
cisco native who has been involved in the fine arts and music scene for over 40 years. He has taught sculp-ture, critical studies and art history at the University of California at Berkley, the San Francisco Art Institute and the Minneapolis College of Art. He has had over 130 solo art exhibi-tions throughout the world. He has 50 public sculptures littered about the American and International landscape. He has collected and studied Art Deco and American and European art pottery for 35 years.His artwork can be seen on his web site: www.corkmarcheschi. com.

DAVID PHIL-LIPS is an international freelance photogra-pher, writer and designer, born in Chile, raised in England and residing, for now, in San Fran-cisco. He is glad now that his schooling included seven years of French which qualified him to work with Cork on this book and led him into various adventures in Paris, Limoges and Alsace, helping research and photographing the fascinating subject of the Atelier Fauré.
More at www.freelancewriterphotographer.com.

This book is for Andrea, Lily, Cara,
Marcel and Luigi.

Marty   Vase Limoges   Fauré Lingtan

                                                        Couvercle
                                                    fil. a 130 m/m 4/10 12 émail
Plaque a   120
185 m/m   121
4/10 émail
fondre le premier   Boîte
mandrin a monter des   lue a 205 m/m 4/10 12 émail
Vases N° 26 à 11   139 m

Marty   Fauré Marty

                                                            88 m

Vase Chateau   N° 181 Monte

                                                    Plaque a 205 m/m 5/
16 x 50
                                                    fondre les mandrin
                                                    monter des Vases et
                                                    grand Champagne
                                                    1er mandrins, 1er —
Marthy

Contents

Foreword

Convergence is at the very center of 20th century culture. The word speaks volumes about the way we perceive works of art today. Art forms, styles, and movements became increasingly intertwined, setting into motion a dizzy array of hybrids—blendings of every imaginable concoction. The advent of collage, photomontage, Duchamp's *Readymades*, Rauschenberg's *Combines*, the shaped canvas, Calder's mobiles, and the introduction of video art are but a few of the innovative breakthroughs. In other disciplines, jazz comes to mind and so too do variations of the blues. In fact, the work of Cork Marcheschi, uniting the wonder of electricity to fine art is but a continuation of what fascinated Emile Gallé. Little wonder that the 20th century offers such a rich vein to explore, an inviting enticement for those individuals wish to wend their way through infinitely complex passages.

A *convergence* of another kind brought Cork Marcheschi and myself together intermittently over the years. We first met in Minneapolis. He was an established artist teaching at the Minneapolis College of Art and Design and I was a curator next door at the Minneapolis Institute of Arts. I was immediately drawn to his work. What he was pursuing seemed to have a sophisticated underpinning, yet offered far more than theory and technical finesse. Our discussions resulted in his modest one-man installation in the museum. In the process I learned that Cork was actively collecting modernist ceramics and glasswork, possessing far more than a passing interest and knowledge of a good many unheralded artisans of the period.

Shortly after the exhibition I was engaged in an ambitious Art Deco exhibition co-organized with Bevis Hillier and presented at the Art Institute in 1971. It consisted of some 1,400 works ranging from flotillas of furniture from Europe to a gallery gleaming with precious jewelry. It had a positive impact on many (including Cork) who were relatively unfamiliar with a large number of the artists represented, not least the work of the Fauré studio. A seed of sorts had been planted.

In 2005, Cork and I began exchanging correspondence revolving around various modern ceramicists. He expressed his continued admiration for the work of Fauré. This culminated in a visit to Cork's San Francisco home on New Year's Day, 2006, sharing dinner with his family and having a long-awaited opportunity to see their ceramics collection. There was considerable discussion about Fauré and it was quite evident that Cork's intense passion would culminate in published material.

While there were extended stretches between our meetings and correspondence over the years, we invariably picked up where we left off, continuing a kind of extended conversation. It stems largely from a common interest: we've been drawn to those artists-architects-designers—past and present—committed to forward-looking designs, those individuals significantly ahead of their time, especially artists who have been virtually ignored over time, yet deserving of re-examination and recognition. It is the basis for Cork's powerful draw to the Fauré aesthetic.

Moreover, Cork has clearly demonstrated to those of us in the museum and academic communities that artists provide an indispensable link in scholarship emanating from hands-on experience—something we, as curators, may overlook and undervalue from time to time. He has confirmed in this study what can be achieved with intellectual curiosity, discipline, perseverance and energy. I know the results of his efforts will serve us well, providing fresh insights and a solid foundation on which to reassess the remarkable work of the Fauré studio.

David Ryan

Curator of Design
Minneapolis Institute of Arts

Introduction

The last studio of the Art Deco period to be researched is that of Camille Fauré. Images of its work are easy to find and the vases are represented in the Louvre, Paris Museum of Decorative Arts, the Victoria and Albert Museum in London, the Minneapolis Institute of the Arts and other museums. They also regularly appear at the major auction houses. But there is no dependable information about the studio. This book answers many questions about the studio's history and its involvement in making modern art inspired vases.

I have given the book a narrow focus. There are many things that this book does not address and I thought it best to let you know what you will and will not find. I do not cover Art Deco enamels by other gifted artisans that practiced in the '20s, '30s and '40s. I also do not cover the entire output of the Fauré studio.

I am concentrating on the Art Deco, geometric, abstract and modernist work that the studio produced. There are a number of fine texts that cover the history of enameling which also cover Gerard Sandoz, Simon Templer, and Jules Sarlandie (to name a few) but none expose the unique work of the Fauré studio.

My interest in this specific body of work stems from a love of early 20th century modern art. It was a heroic period filled with energy, enthusiasm, ideas and great work. Think about the impact of Futurism, Cubism, Dada, the Russian avant-garde, the Orphic painters all the way through Abstract Expressionism. WOW! That is an amazing 50 year period!

Fauré, more than any other group of artisans, embraced modern art. Most other studios leaned heavily on tradition and shared a lot of the same imagery (think seascapes in Carmel). Fauré produced art objects of great presence and power. They did not pay homage to the past and they did not try to change tradition. What they did do is produce a new art that had never been seen before.

If you look at the American art pottery of Newcomb, Grueby, Rookwood, Marblehead, etc., you will see that the imagery is very naturalistic and conservative. There are few risks taken. R. Guy Cowan studied in Paris, and he brought that experience with him back to Cowan pottery, but Cowan's nod to modernist themes was slight. Victor Schreckengost's Jazz Bowl was the most adventurous Cowan got.

Roseville had a brief flirtation with their Futura line. Futura (1928) was the work of one designer, Frank Ferrel. I don't think Ferrel had much contact with the modern art world. He designed his concept of "modernistic" for the Futura line. If you look at Futura in relationship to the output of Roseville, it is obvious that an attempt was being made to replicate images that Ferrell had seen in periodicals, without the benefit of understanding the work itself. Consequently some Futura has an awkward feel to it and some of it is innocently delightful.

Fauré is unique because it was of the Modern Art moment and Andrée Fauré was well aware of her sources. Another unique thing about Fauré's pieces of this style and period is their objectness. These enameled vases were sat with and focused on for extended periods of time. The laborious and impossibly exacting skill to produce one of these vases required the artisan to be in a meditative state; there is no other way to do what needs to be done. In the interview with Mauricette Pinoteau, who worked in the studio in the 1970s, she speaks of time being transformed and of entering a world of elegant pleasure. This reward had to be strong because the workers who produced these pieces were poorly compensated.

This is why I have decided to concentrate on this specific work alone. The much larger body of the Fauré studio's output is very good but not extraordinary or different in any way from other studios.

If you go to Limoges, France today and visit one of the local enamelers you will find the type of imagery being produced that has been created for over 100 years. But you will not find the daring and dramatic modernist work of studio C. Fauré.

Cork Marcheschi
San Francisco, June 2006

The Jazz Bowl by Viktor Schreckengost for Cowan Pottery commissioned by Eleanor Roosevelt ca.1930, New York (Jones collection, Florida.).

Roseville Futura line, introduced 1928. (Collection of the author.)

American Art pots. L-R Marblehead, (gold) Grueby, Van Briggle, Newcomb.

The Journey

In the summer of 2005, the American Society of Enamelists asked me to give a lecture on the work of Camille Fauré at their annual convention. I was more than happy to have the opportunity to share an accumulation of information gathered over 30 years of researching, poking around and picking up rumors.

While speaking to the gathering of enamelists the question came up more than a few times: "How did you gather this information?"

It's a long story and before I answer that question it may be of interest to know that I seem to have a DNA marker that wants to see original and genuine talent recognized. When I see history take the easy way out I get upset. Before my research on Fauré, I championed two other artists and brought their work to light. In 1995 I produced the first album that the jazz great, Oscar Brown Junior, had made in 20 years. In 2004 I wrote a piece for Modernism Magazine on John Foster, the one-handed modernist potter from Detroit. I have now turned my attention to the mystery of the Fauré studio.

In 1970 I left my home in San Francisco to take a job as a sculpture teacher at the Minneapolis College of Art and Design. Up to that point, my only knowledge of Minnesota was a line from a Frank Zappa song: "Gonna freak out in Minnesota!" I had to get an atlas to find Minneapolis. I never planned to leave the Bay Area, but neither had I planned to have a child and wife (#1) at 25 years old. So I packed the U-Haul and away we went.

I was offered a rental home across the street from the Minneapolis Institute of the Arts, the parent organization for the art school, and a world class museum. I unpacked the family in upper Midwestern humidity and quickly learned about the feasting habits of the local 10,000 Lakes mosquito (the Minnesota state bird!).

My sculptures were well received in Minneapolis, and in '71 I was invited to be in the opening exhibition of the new Walker Art Center. David Ryan was, and is, Curator at the Minneapolis Institute. He saw my work at the Walker and offered me a show.

Dunand bowl (Morgan collection, Kansas City, MO.).

Chevron shoes (Private collection).

Christofle vase 1925 (collection of the author).

During the same period that my show was up at the Art Institute, America's first major Art Deco exhibition was also showing.

My artwork was electrical and mechanical and needed frequent attention, so I was often at the museum. After repairing my artwork I would wander through the Deco show. On my first pass through, it was a pair of '30s era shoes with chevrons cut into them that got my attention. They were out of a cartoon. I loved them! Upon subsequent visits my focus became sharper. The eggshell and lacquer work of Dunand, the electroplated copper and silver pieces by Christoffle.

Then the works of two artists crept to the forefront of my many visits. These pieces were the very funny and exotic Futurist cats of Louis Wain from 1914, and the enamel vases of Atelier Camille Fauré. After a while I would return only to spend time with the Wains and Faurés–very different pieces and very different artists.

Louis Wain Futurist Cats, 1914 (collection of the author).

Louis Wain might be the subject of another book. For now I want to concentrate on Fauré. These enamel pieces possessed a vibrancy I'd never seen in objects of art before. To say the pieces were bright is an understatement. They emitted a crisply defined radiance. The only thing I had ever experienced that had a bit of that was a freshly coated candy apple illuminated by a full summer sun. You can see the surface of the red cinnamon candy and feel its depth as the light penetrates the glazing and reflects off the apple. The Fauré vases also did this and much more. Beyond this amazing presence there was a sense of exuberant play and zaniness that to me captured the spirit of the moment in which they were created. These art objects were the essential "anything can happen" children of the Art Deco spirit. Fearless!

So I looked. I gazed. I wondered. What are these things? Who is the artist and how are they made? As a sculptor I had broad familiarity with materials and I

The Fauré vases on display at the Minneapolis Institute of the Arts exhibition in 1971.

knew enough about enamels, glass, metal and heat to intuit that these were impossible objects! The worm had turned for me, and a desire to learn and acquire was born.

The early '70s were a golden age for collecting. There was, as yet, no Antiques Road Show, no Kovel's syndicated articles, no antique malls of any consequence, no Schiffer books and no eBay. On any Saturday and Sunday you could find Knights of Columbus fund-raisers, church bazaars and shopping mall collectible weekends. Hummels ruled the landscape! The Antique Trader was the newsprint paper out of Grundy Center, Iowa that was just pages of classified ads. I would await the arrival of the Trader and quickly go through the china/pottery "for sale" section. I found wonderful pieces of Cowan, Futura, Longway and SEG, but no Camille Fauré.

Over the next several years I was fortunate: I got a divorce and my art career took off.

By 1973 I had wife #2, Donna, and galleries: in New York, the Louis K. Meisel Gallery; Kansas City, The Morgan Gallery; San Francisco, Modernism; and Gallery M in Germany. Everywhere I went to show my sculpture I also picked through local collectibles' shops or antique shops.

In 1978 I was awarded the DAAD, an artist fellowship in Berlin, Germany. My wife and I were hosted for one year, all expenses paid, plus a monthly stipend and a museum exhibition. Upon getting this information, my first course of action was to gather addresses of all the Deco shops and flea markets in Paris, London, Holland and Belgium. I bought maps and talked with antique dealers and museum curators I had gotten to know. I was going to be ready for a year of deep collecting and making some of my own work for a show at the National Gallery in Berlin. I was pumped for this!

(Both pages) Fauré vases from
the Brohan collection, Berlin.

Upon arriving in Berlin I was pleased to find out that I really was an invited guest of
the government and that in Germany artists are treated with respect, something that is
sadly lacking in America. The DAAD would facilitate introductions and make things
happen for me, if they could.

The place in Berlin that I wanted access to was the Samlung Brohan, or in English, the
Brohan Collection, a private museum of decorative arts. It is a great collection that was
put together at a time before other museums were taking the decorative arts of the early
20th century seriously. The DAAD created an introduction for me and I got to spend
time with the best of the Deco period. This was my first opportunity to handle Fauré
vases and to get some information on where they came from. If you are ever in Berlin
and have any interest in this period of design, the Brohan Collection is a must see. I
saw five pieces of Fauré at the museum. They were even more beautiful than I remem-

bered the pieces in Minneapolis to be. WOW! The surfaces were pristine. The colors were complex. The light play could only happen with these materials. Then there is the surface. The enamels are dimensionally built up. The raised area has crisp edges and up to ½ inch lift off the surface of the vase. This isn't possible! In traditional enameling the material melts, just like butter in an oven. So how can these complex forms have defined edges and be of different thicknesses, defying thermal shock, and still be in one piece???

I asked these questions in the tone of voice of a 14-year-old boy with his first crush. The answer was beautifully worded, "This is not known!" (Say that like Colonel Clink from Hogan's Heroes TV show and you've got it.) How is it that work of this significance has no history? Museums are usually ripe with more detail than you could ever absorb. But not this time.

The two Fauré vases I bought from Alain
Lesieutre in Paris in 1978. (Vase on right
attributed to M. Rozier, vase on left to
Lucie Dada, design and execution.)

One of the other artists on the DAAD was Ed Kienholz. I had admired Ed's work since the LA County Museum show in 1965. It was fun getting to know Ed and his wife Nancy. We would hang out in his studio drinking cheap Italian wine (delivered weekly in 5-gallon jugs). One afternoon over some sachertorte, I mentioned that I was planning a trip to Paris to do the flea markets and to see the Deco dealer Alain Lesieutre. "FLEA MARKETS!" Ed responded. "You know about the flea markets?" Yes, I answered, and before the end of the sachertorte, Ed had called his travel agent and booked flights and hotel rooms. We would all be going to Paris the following week.

We arrived in Paris and were greeted by a friendly hotel staff who clearly knew Ed from previous stays. This was fun. The next day we went to see Alain Lesieutre's shop. I was excited. He was the dealer who lent the Fauré pieces to the Minneapolis Institute show. I was two blocks away when I spotted his shop. In the front window were at least six Fauré pieces. I was told by Ed, Nancy and Donna that my posture changed, my pace quickened and something happened to me that was palpable.

Mr.. Lesieutre's shop was beautiful. Only the best was on display and for sale: Dunand, Marinot, McKnight Kauffer, Christoffle, and several Faurés. The four of us entered the shop and I tried not to babble. I looked at everything and, after being invited to touch, I held and touched everything.

We spent about 90 minutes talking with Mr.. Lesieutre. I bought two pieces from the 1930's. It wasn't until 20 years latter that I found out that these pieces were actually made in the late '60s.

The Faurés became the objects of constant fascination. Every opportunity I had, I asked about them and their maker, but for 25 years nothing useful came to me. There were rumors of Camille Fauré's widow bootlegging his work. If you had the skill, technique, facility and design sense to copy the work, more power to ya! We aren't talking about plaster molds for slip casting that can be pulled off a Weller vase. This is more akin to playing Rachmaninoff with the skill and passion of Van Cliburn.

Slowly I started to make inroads into the mystery of the Fauré enamels and I was surprised by what I found.

In 1992 a show of Art Deco enamels (Emaux Art Deco Biennale) was assembled in

Limoges. Gérard Malabre, Camille Fauré's grandson, was very much involved in putting the show together. The show featured a history of most of the important enamelers of the period and had the best examples of Fauré pieces seen in many years. The accompanying booklet was written by Limoges scholar, Michel Kiener, and covers the subject well. Unfortunately this catalog is out of print and very difficult to find. It didn't make it into my hands until 2002 . I went online and searched for Michel Kiener and found a few links. I sent him a note with an apology for not writing in French and telling him about my desire to write a book about Fauré. About a month later Mr.. Kiener wrote back, a very friendly letter in English. He answered a few of my questions. I responded with more questions, and in another month came another response. It became clear that a trip to Limoges was necessary.

I do not speak French and I am not a professional photographer. I needed both and found them in David Phillips, one of my better finds on Craigslist! David and I met, got along, and started planning a research and photographic expedition. David made a contact within the city government of Limoges.

A very kind and helpful person took interest in this project and made some local inquiries for me. I had asked about use of images from the Emaux Art Deco book. She made quick headway and got in touch with the people who controlled the images.

I am not sure who those people are, as I never got the photos. My ally in the Limoges government started to hit some road blocks. The easy prospect of getting permission to scan some images or get some transparencies started to get murky. The museum wouldn't return her calls and my questions about contacting collectors were being ignored. Michel Kiener wasn't responding to my e-mails, and David was set to go to Limoges to document artwork. Finally David made contact with one of the photographers who shot the Emaux Art Deco catalog. Nice guy, happy to help, but another author had just been by and bought the photos I needed.

This other author is a South American antique dealer who collects objects and then writes a book about them, which in turn raises their value in the market. Then he schedules an auction or some other type of sale. We were definitely writing different books, but it doesn't matter when you are after the same info. Through the Decodence Gallery in San Francisco, who are specialists in Fauré, I was put in contact with another

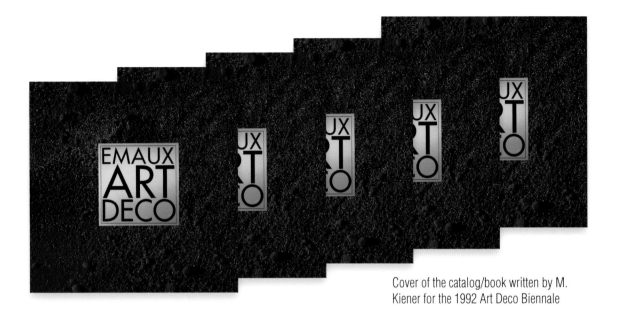

Cover of the catalog/book written by M. Kiener for the 1992 Art Deco Biennale

person who had expressed interest in writing a Fauré book.

I contacted Lucien Geismar in France. I was so pleased when I got an e-mail back from Lucien. He was very open and had a great collection of Fauré. Half the pieces in the Emaux Art Deco catalog came from his collection. He said he would be happy to have his work photographed. He also recommended that we contact a friend of his in Paris. According to Lucien, this Parisian private collector had the BEST collection! So the private collector in Paris was contacted and an appointment was set to visit his collection. One other appointment was made, and that was with the Edmond Allain company. These are the people who produced all of Fauré's copper forms starting in 1919. So with three appointments in France and many question marks in Limoges, an expedition was launched.

In the United States I had already photographed the Bill and Jan Jones collection of 65 pieces. The private Paris collection produced great pictures of fabulous Faurés. The remainder of the pieces in the Emaux Art Deco catalog were in this other collection. Why hadn't the people at the local museum or Michel Kiener told me about these collections? They were both in the 1992 showing.

Next stop Limoges. The director of the Évêché Museum was very evasive and wouldn't

(Right)
Vast Jones collection
of Fauré vases, Florida.

(Left and below)
Private collection in
France.

(Left and below)
The collection of Fauré
vases and sketches of a Paris
collector

(Right)
Some of the Lucien Geismar collection , France.

(Below)
Two Fauré and an Henriette Marty vase in a Limoges antique shop, a rare sight these days.

City Hall, Limoges.

Musée de L'Évêché with a small Fauré collection.

Porcelain fountain in front of City Hall

Bridge over river Vienne with St. Etienne Cathedral in background

commit to an appointment. We didn't feel like kissing the Pope's ring, so we politely blew the director off. Michel Kiener showed up and wanted to tag along to see the Geismar collection–mind you this is a 14 hour round-trip drive.

It became apparent that Limoges has at least two warring Masonic lodges. Apparently these lodges are quite powerful and work behind the scenes in city government and city cultural affairs. I had made the mistake of talking to members of both lodges, which pissed everybody off. Members of one lodge do not deal with members of another. If you want a government job that will raise you above middle management you must join a lodge.

While in Limoges it became clear that the Masons had a lock on certain information, and also that the South American author had paid for exclusive interviews and photographs and consequently I could not re-interview these people. This book is about some

St. Etienne Cathedral, Limoges.

Limoges shop of Paul Bufforn, enameller who worked in the Fauré studio in the '70s.

interesting vases, not the search for DNA! The sense of intrigue was palpable.

I then found out a local historian was also writing a book about Fauré. This Limoges author would write a very scholarly treatise on the Atelier Fauré.

The Boulevard Louis Blanc is the porcelain and enamel row of Limoges. Every other store is selling porcelain or enamels. A chance meeting led to the discovery of Mauricette Pinoteau, whose shop is on Louis Blanc. Her enameling is the only contemporary work that has echoes of Fauré. She turned out to be a delightful woman who worked for 6 years for Andrée Fauré and had been schooled by one of the Fauré masters in the Art Deco technique. She was willing to talk and to share.

Mauricette loved enameling and she had great praise for Andrée Fauré.

Along with my 150 images of amazing vases, Mauricette Pinoteau provided the answers to most of my questions, and the research was nearly done. Following in the same vein

Mauricette Pinoteau, former employee of Andrée Fauré Malabre in the Atelier Fauré during the 1970s, one of two or three people who can still produce the Art Deco Fauré style enamel vases (these are her vases shown below, Jones collection, Florida).
Mauricette's studio/shop is at 6 Boulevard Louis Blanc, 87000 Limoges, France.
E-mail: perlesdekaolin@orange.fr.

of happenstance, another person, who must remain anonymous, had a large collection of original drawings by Andrée Fauré as well as the pounce patterns for the Deco Fauré vases. This anonymous collector was very gracious and let the images be photographed. With this stroke of luck my research was completed.

In the next two years, three books about Studio Fauré will be released, each with a very distinct voice. I look forward to seeing what I have missed.

I have been an aficionado of Blues and Jazz for most of my life. This music is based on the oral tradition which states that you must be in the same space with the music as it is being created in order for you to be changed by it. I have found this sensibility to be very true in my life. Things don't happen unless you put yourself out there.

The safety of an internet connection can only take you so far. The good stuff doesn't start to happen until you have exhausted all of the safe and secure avenues and all arrows point to a clearly defined question mark.

Hold your breath, flush your rational mind and go!

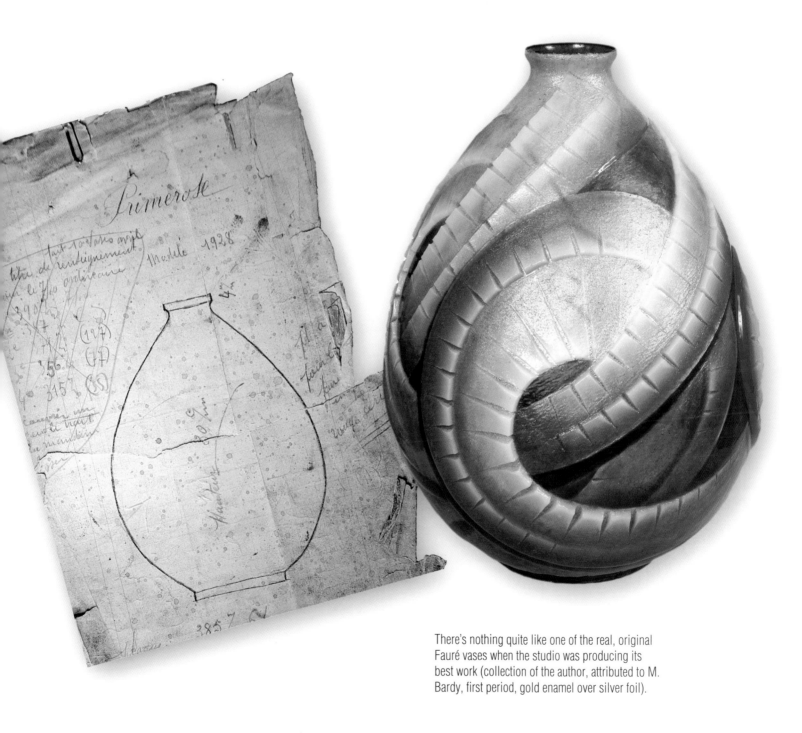

There's nothing quite like one of the real, original Fauré vases when the studio was producing its best work (collection of the author, attributed to M. Bardy, first period, gold enamel over silver foil).

The Art Deco Cocktail

Art is an area of endeavor that people feel very free to offer strong opinions about. The axiom, "I know what I like, and I don't like that," is actually a misstatement. What is normally being said is, "I like what I know, and I don't know that."

Art, science, the law, medicine and carpentry all have a language and craft that is studied and learned. Why people won't offer art the same respect as these other professions is crazy making.

To appreciate the moment of foment that was Fauré, you need to be willing to entertain some minor art historical information. I have attempted in this chapter to offer an introduction to a few of Andrée Fauré's major influences (Andrée was Camille Fauré's daughter who was the creative influence behind the Fauré studio and managed it for many years).

This light dusting of art history will allow for a deeper appreciation of the Atelier Fauré's artworks.

Enter the Camera, Exit Realism

Up until the camera was developed, it was the artist's job to replicate reality in a realistic way. The images that we have of people, places and things from before 1850 were the work of artists, doing what artists did before we had a tool that did it faster, cheaper and more accurately. With the advent of photography artists weren't out of a job. Hardly! They were free to develop an understanding of other realities.

The Impressionists were the first group of artists to allow science to affect their process. An understanding of how the rods and cones in the eye functioned, along with photographic freedom, set these guys free. They broke up the image into dabs of paint that only formed an image at a distance. A question was being asked about what it is that we think we see and what it is that we actually perceive. These pictures are easily beautiful, but they also have content beyond their beauty.

Graphic reproduction in acrylics of Impressionist painting by Pierre Bonnard done by Pamela Holm, San Francisco..

Graphic reproduction of 1914 painting by Futurist Giacomo Balla done by Pamela Holm, San Francisco.

Italy. The Futurists!

Try to imagine what it must have been like to be a contemporary artist in Italy in 1909. More than any other country, the weight of antiquity was stifling. From this pressure of tradition and resistance to change sprung the most dynamic Modern Art movement of the 20th Century. On Feb. 20, 1909, Fillipo Tomaso Marinetti published the first manifesto of Futurism:

> "Let's go, say I! Let's go, friends! Let's go!…
> A speeding automobile is more beautiful than
> The winged victory!"

Long Live Italy, 1912 by Futurist Giacomo Balla (private collection).

Detail from painting , *Bird's Movement*, 1913 by Futurist Fortunato Depero (Rovereto, Museo d'Arte Moderna e Contemporanea di Trento e Rovereto).

Study for painting, *Dancer=Propeller=Sea*, 1914, by Futurist Gino Severini (private collection, Minnesota).

And from the first manifesto of Futurist painting:

> "Destroy the cult of the past, the obsession of the antique.
> Take and glorify the life of today, incessantly and tumultuously
> transformed by the triumphs of science."

In 1909 there was no TV, no radio, no movies. Art was an active part of the culture. You can't make any comparison to our oversaturated, undereducated, fame addicted present day culture. The Futurists scandalized all of Europe. This group of artists brought their art movement to the streets and nightclubs of Italy. They pamphleted their manifestos on street corners and challenged everything that was safe and traditional—they were a fun group of guys!

Graphic reproduction of painting by Fernand Léger by Pamela Holm (San
Francisco), and Fauré vase (Lucien Geismar collection, France).

The Futurists' paintings and sculptures attempted to show the effect of energy on its
subject. One of the most famous paintings is of a dog being walked on a leash. The
leash and dog's feet are in motion. Images of music and light also attempted to demon-
strate the synchronicity and interpenetration of light, sound, music and energy. Try to
envision a quiet room with steam rising from a cup of hot tea. Now slowly drag your
hand through the rising steam: you can watch the vertical column of water vapor break
into opposed spirals in space. This is a simple visual cue about the unseen world we live
in that the Futurist wanted to make visible. You can see how the visual structure of their
paintings became an inspiration for Andrée Fauré.

Fauré vase compared to graphic reproduction of Futurist painting by Balla,
done by Pamela Holm, San Francisco (vases Brohan collection, Berlin).

Several of the Futurist compositions show up very clearly in Fauré designs.

World War I

We had never had a world war before. This was new and different. In this war we were introduced to trench warfare, mustard gas that blistered lungs and burned flesh, and the first use of airplanes in combat. It was a world gone mad.

To make things really strange, the Swiss decided not to participate in World War I. They became a neutral country. No war in Switzerland. They knew they had to protect their store of cuckoo clocks and cheese. Because of this neutral status, Zurich became

Dada posters (private collection, Berlin).

Künstlerkneipe Voltaire
Allabendlich (mit Ausnahme von Freitag)
Musik-Vorträge und Rezitationen
Eröffnung Samstag den 5. Februar
im Saale der „Meierei" Spiegelgasse 1

a new home for artists, musicians, dramatists, poets, and creative people from around the world. This little town was bursting with an international group of artists that didn't support the madness of the war.

Hugo Ball, from Germany, frequented a local bar called Cabaret Voltaire. He asked the owner of the bar if he could advertise a literary evening one night a week. The idea took off and soon Cabaret Voltaire was the place for artists of all types to hang out. In response to the war, these artists felt they could not make art that was sane or pleasant. They needed to make absurd art, anti-art, to match the madness of the world that was killing itself just miles away. So in 1916 a letter opener was slipped into a dictionary,

Meret Openheim's *Fur Lined Teacup* (collection of Museum of Modern Art, New York City).

Teatime by Cubist Jean Metzinger, 1911 (private collection, New York City).

the book was opened and the word the letter opener pointed to was "Dada," French for "hobby horse." With that gesture, Dada was formally born.

The public responded to Dada and Futurism by rioting at a number of their exhibitions and destroying artwork. How refreshing it must have been to have an engaged audience. A very famous piece of sculpture by Meret Oppenheim is a Fur Lined Teacup. This absurd sculpture sums up the response to the absurdity of war.

At this same time you had Picasso, Braque, and Gris (in Paris) developing Analytical Cubism. This was the reduction of the image to its basic geometric planes. The work of

Magazine Section
Part Six

The New York Times.

SUNDAY, MARCH 16, 1913.

Magazine Section
Part Six

"CUBISTS AND FUTURISTS ARE MAKING INSANITY PAY"

SEEING NEW YORK WITH A CUBIST

The Rude Descending a Staircase
(Rush Hour at the Subway)

Newspaper cartoonists had a field day with the Armory Show. One (*above*) saw Duchamp's *Nude* as inspired by the subway rush hour. Another insisted that the old ladies who made patchwork quilts originated Cubism. The soundest comment came from an editorial writer who warned, "You can't spoof what you don't understand."

THE ORIGINAL CUBIST

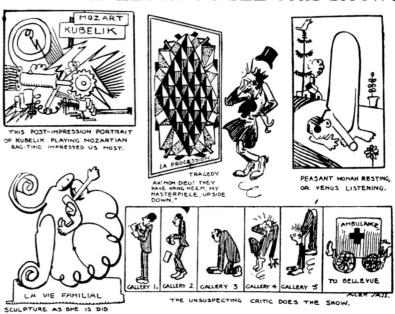

Feb. 17, 1913

NOBODY WHO HAS BEEN DRINKING IS LET IN TO SEE THIS SHOW.

these artists is well represented in most museums about the world. Cubism is also the school of modern art that is most frequently made visual fun of in comic strips or even cartoons. Putting two eyes and both ears on one side of the nose is a common visual joke at Cubism's expense.

At the same time in Russia there were the Constructivists and Suprematists. These groups were very interested in the organization of the picture plane in geometric compositions. Rectangles, squares and straight lines are displayed in energetic compositions. After the Revolution their work was not allowed to be publicly shown in Russia until the Berlin wall came down. The fear of a few geometric forms was astounding. These

Gouache study for Disks, 1912, by Robert Delaunay (Moreno collection, Minnesota).

Painting by Russian Suprematist Kasimir Malevich (courtesy of Morton Newman archive, Chicago).

Vase by Gustav Heinkel of the Bauhaus (collection of the Minneapolis Institute of the Arts)

Fauré vase, (Lucien Geismar collection, France).

Suprematist compositions were also an influence on Fauré.

The Bauhaus in Germany changed the world of design. Their attitude toward design as content is still relevant and current today. Many of the pieces of furniture that came out of the Bauhaus still appear weekly in modernist homes featured in architectural magazines.

Finally we have the school of Paris, which included many artists including Fernand Leger, Sonia and Robert Delaunay, and Kandinsky. They were all very influential to Fauré, and their influence is easily identified. Delaunay and Leger laid down the ground work for the

Posters from the 1925 Paris Fair (private collection, New York).

most successful designs ever created by Fauré.

The Industrial Revolution, war, war profiteering, young people entering a new age, and the end of World War I. Let's have a party!

All of this was going on between 1909 and 1925. The images of this art appeared in newspapers and magazines. The 1925 fair in Paris had an entire section of current abstract art. Henriette Marty and Andrée Fauré were young women who were thrilled and inspired by all of this energy. There was a collective desire to escape the past and discover the new. The celebration that we know as Art Deco was about to erupt!

MINISTERE DU COMMERCE ET DE L'INDUSTRIE

☆ PAR LABEUR & PAR GENIE

EXPOSITION INTERNATIONALE
DES ARTS DECORATIFS
ET INDUSTRIELS MODERNES
PARIS AVRIL-OCTOBRE 1925

MINISTÈRE DU COMMERCE ET DE L'INDUSTRIE

PARIS·1925

EXPOSITION
INTERNATIONALE
DES ARTS DÉCORATIFS
ET INDUSTRIELS
MODERNES
AVRIL- OCTOBRE

The 1925 fair in Paris is pointed to as the watershed event that defined the Art Deco moment. One very important point about the structure of the fair was its stated requirement that the work to be shown had to be new, of the moment and pointing to the future. This created the situation where some established designers' work fell outside the guidelines and they were not given prime view in the fair. The other important point to consider is post-war optimism, new money in new hands, and a celebration of luxury, opulence and extravagance. These were good times for people who were making expensive decorative objects.

These art movements and moments are the seeds from which sprouted the inspiration

Fauré vases (Brohan collection, Berlin).

of the Art Deco designers. Then, in a more accessible form, the designers presented their interpretations to the public.

Atelier Fauré's work was met with some of the same animosity as the avant-garde art movements.

Even with the beautiful surfaces that the Fauré vases presented, the power of the abstract art ideas was still too strong for many. Here is a quote form a 1930 critic's review:

"…but why do all of our enamelers believe they must weigh down certain of their works with a bony thickness, notably with layers of opal that bring to mind slices of lard, and

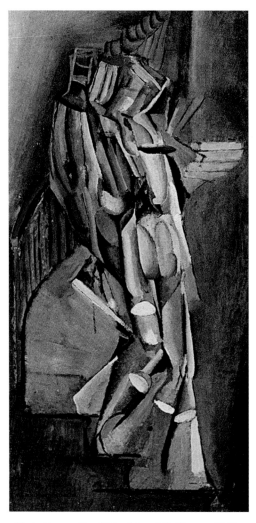

Nude Descending Stairs, Marcel DuChamp, 1912
(collection of the Philadelphia Museum of Art).

Untitled, Jackson Pollack (private collection, Germany).

make their vases resemble, if only they were of a blood-like color, knuckles of ham decked out by some art-loving butcher? Who is the homicidal Hun who has told them that this was modern?" Limousine criticism is harsh.

Other great moments in art criticism: when Marcel Duchamp showed *Nude Descending the Staircase* at the 1913 Armory show in NYC, his work was referred to as "an explosion in a shingle factory." In the early 1950s, American abstract expressionist painter Jackson Pollack was referred to as "Jack the Dripper."

Atelier Fauré

Camille Fauré was born in 1872 in Périgueux, of the same family as the musician Gabriel Fauré. He apprenticed with his father in the sign painting trade, and when he returned from fighting in WW I, moved to Limoges and set up shop there, the Camille Fauré sign painting studio. Limoges was and is a conservative city. It holds its history dear to its heart and has not made any attempt to eagerly move into the 20th century–forget about the 21st. Outside of France, Limoges is best known for its porcelains and enamelware. Within France it is also known as the beef center of the country. The town also has several very well established and rival Masonic Lodges, as you will discover if you try to do any serious research or business there.

Camille Fauré's company painted decorative signs and carts. He was successful and his business thrived. Living in Limoges, it was impossible for anyone to avoid the underglazed ceramics for which the city had been famous for centuries. In the early days of Rookwood, the underglazed technique was referred to as Cincinnati Limoges. Enameling had also had a long and well-established history in Limoges.

These two industries needed many craftspeople to produce their wares, so there was a large pool of skilled artisans. This was kind of like working at the Ford plant if you were born in Detroit or, more appropriately, carving marble if you were born in Carrarra or Pietra Santa in Italy. The specific skill in Limoges was working with slip, a muddy glaze that was applied to porcelain vessels, or the mud-like enamels that were applied to copper plates or copper vessels. The other unique skill was knowing how to translate flat art to the volumes of the vessels.

Fauré was aware that the traditional enameling techniques and imagery were beginning to change. Local artists such as Leon Jouhaud, Jules Sarlandie and Roger and Charles Peltant were producing unique plaques, plates and small vessels with a contemporary feel. (These artists' work are covered very well in Michel Kiener's EMAUX ART DECO.) This was definitely a nod that the past had finally started to loose its grip .

Fauré store front 31 Rue des Tanneries, Limoges.

The original, pre-war charcoal kiln.

In 1919 Fauré decided to diversify and opened a shop for decorative enamels. It is important to note that he was not involved creatively in any aspects of this new venture other than being the proprietor. It was his business and it bore his name. He hired Raphael Bétourné from Paris, but from the beginning there was a clash of ideology. His new hire was limited by the weight and traditions of the past. He wasn't going to be the artist to break with tradition. Fauré had some undefined ideas about something new starting to happen. He didn't know what, but felt that the time was ripe for change. Fauré got very lucky when he partnered up with a well-established pair of enamel artists, Alexandre Marty (1876-1943) and his daughter, Henriette (1902-1992).

Vases and brooch by Henriette Marty (signature below)
(collection Lucien Geismar, France).

Marty was 50 years old and had extensive experience in the ceramic underglazing techniques of Limoges. He wanted to learn the technique of enameling, but found that the major practitioners of the city were very tight lipped about their secrets, and Marty was left to fend for himself. Secrets play a large part of this story. This was the best thing that could have happened to Marty and Fauré. Marty's energetic curiosity led him to develop direct flame and drip techniques as well as his most important discovery, the ability to sculpturally build up the surface of the vase with thick enamel. There would be no Fauré Art Deco vases without the contribution of Alexandre Marty.

This is where things start to get interesting. Marty was a master craftsman and matched

Vase by Alexandre Marty, 1924 (collection Lucien Geismar, France).

Fauré in his desire for something new, but unlike Fauré, the businessman, Marty had the technical skill and a voracious curiosity to make it happen. Marty was an enthusiastic experimenter and hired gun. Marty was very much like the hot glass artisans of Murano, Italy, and more recently Seattle, Washington, where skilled craftsmen are always needed by some studio. Marty's skill was so great that his name graces many pieces designed by others but brought to reality by Marty in spectacular fashion. Marty's daughter was a good designer, educated artist and aware of the current Modernist art movements. The Martys showed work in the 1925 Paris Exposition. It was a near disaster as their crate of vases was lost in transit. They were able to regroup and remake

Andrée Fauré applying silver foil to a copper vase.

the pieces for the show. Upon return from the 1925 Paris exhibition the Martys were so taken with the modern movement that they completely redid their house in the Art Deco style and that decor remained until Henriette's death.

It was Marty's creative experimentation that gave Fauré enamels their distinct three-dimensional surfaces. The technique that Marty developed was not a scientific or technical development; it was a subtle intuitive relationship to his material and the magic of the fire.

As mentioned, Camille Fauré also had a daughter, Andrée (1904-1985). When she was

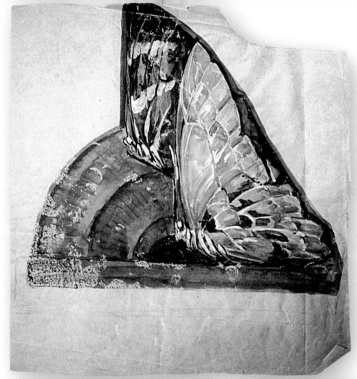

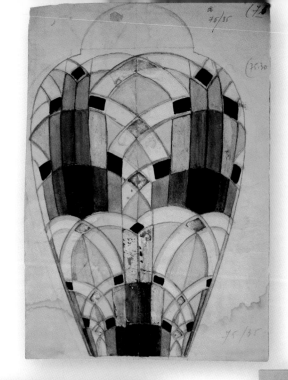

14 years old she contracted a serious illness that required a year of bed rest. During her recuperation her father encouraged her to draw and paint. He supplied drawing and painting materials. This was the beginning of Andrée's life as an artist/designer. Andrée went to art school (École Des Beaux Arts) in Limoges and was formally trained. Henriette Marty also went to the same school. More important than this rigorous training was Andrée's exposure to the most exciting period in modern art history. She loved it and was able to assimilate all the modern styles. In 1923 Camille brought his staff, including Andrée, to the Colonial Exposition in Paris. This was a very powerful experience for all concerned. Even though this show didn't have the full Art Deco impact that

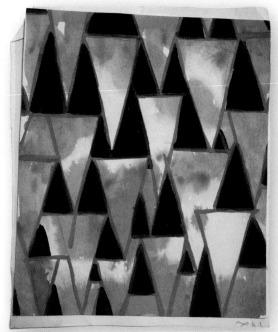

the 1925 fair would, it still had the modern movement very present and its relationship to earlier periods was obvious. The Art Nouveax period with its muted colors and whiplash lines was officially over. Bold color and defined line replaced the soft focus and muted tones. This trip would also be the Atelier Fauré's only contact with Paris. From here on out, Lyon would be their center for commerce.

Unfortunately there wasn't enough business in the studio to support the partnership of Marty and Fauré so Henriette and Alexandre left Fauré in 1924. It is interesting to think what might have happened if they could have stuck it out one more year and entered the magic of 1925.

1927 Andrée Fauré watercolor and resulting vase (painting now in private collection, France and vase in Brohan Collection, Berlin.)

By this time the techniques of thick, dimensional enamels that Marty developed were part of the Fauré studio, and five budding masters had been trained in the technique, but it would be another three years before the fledgling masters could gain enough control to produce hard-edged designs with consistent accuracy. At 20 years old, Andrée had become the designer for the atelier. Her father gave her carte blanche. This is historically a rare moment when commerce actually helped create a unique and important art statement. As long as the shop was profitable Andrée could do anything she liked. Camille preferred to be hunting, spending time on his farm and tending his cows. Seeing that Limoges sprouted no contemporary art scene (actually quite the contrary),

1930 Andrée Fauré watercolor and resulting vase, (watercolor in private collection, France and vase in Sonnabend Collection, New York).

Andrée constantly looked at magazines that featured modern art. From this secondhand exposure she developed inspired designs that informed a unique language in a process that had never existed.

Andrée understood the materials and knew the techniques. I can't express what a feat it was for Andrée to be able to understand the artwork that she used for inspiration. The simple-minded application of motif or pattern is always visible as a thin veneer that only hints at a deeper possibility that the designer does not comprehend. She was able to design for vessels in a way that incorporated the thick enamel into the fabric of the design. It wasn't just a visual trick or gimmick. A less talented artist would not have

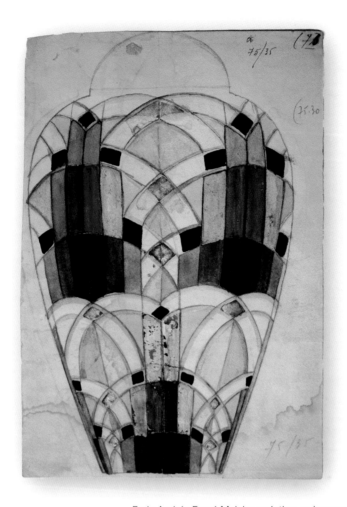 

Early Andrée Fauré Malabre painting and corresponding vase (probably a later reproduction)
(sketch in private collection, Limoges, France and vase in Jones collection, Florida).

been able to gracefully make the translation. Andrée was the architect with a vision and the master made it happen.

A subtle point that should not be underappreciated is Andrée's use of color. She used the colors that were being used by the modern painters: strong and pure, not diffuse or muted. It was a radical gesture to place a bright red geometric form against a jet black geometric form and float them in a field of bright white. I realize it doesn't sound like a bold step, but in 1924 Limoges it was near heresy. The next 15 years (1925-1940) were the years that the designs of Andrée and Atelier Fauré would create the body of work that is now found in decorative arts collections in museums around the world. Bold,

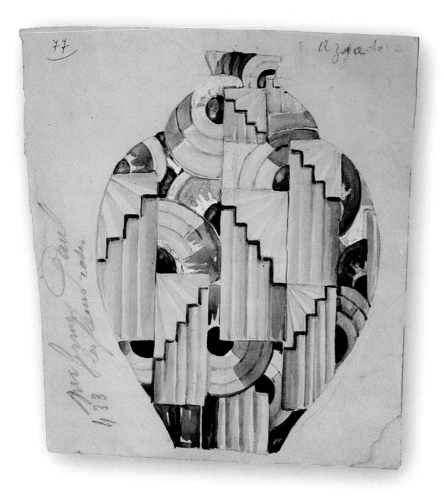

Andrée Fauré Malabre sketch and corresponding vase (sketch in private collection, Limoges, France and vase in Sonnabend collection, New York City).

daring, dramatic and wildly exuberant, it is easy to see the influences of Cubism, Futurism, the Russian Suprematist, Fernand Léger, Robert and Sonia Delaunay (as discussed in Chapter 2) and the studio's own willingness to go for it. This period produced some of the most stunning examples of Art Deco objects ever to be made. The studio also produced some of the most zany and exotic designs. When I look at these more extreme pieces I want to know WHAT WERE THEY THINKING ABOUT? These objects really take chances and push limits. They need to be looked at under a focus that is other than the Art Deco filter. To have fun and play with modern art can be disastrous, but what was done in the studio was outrageously inspired!

Early Fauré vase (private collection, France).

Unlike the studios of Paris where designers and decorators were part and parcel of the moment, the Fauré studio was a blue collar operation that had no salon and wasn't part of a chichi society scene. History favors the easy to document. In Paris the wealthy collectors, salon society critics and writers were part of the same circle. This type of incestuous relationship still exists and severely limits the NEW from ever surfacing naturally. This is common in most creative endeavors.

If you were a great sax player in 1950 with ideas that made a brand new sound but lived in Omaha, the chances are these ideas would remain unheard unless you took them to New York and played where the focus of the jazz world was. The same was true for

Atelier Fauré–Limoges and Omaha have a lot in common. In the real world if you are not making your art happen under the limited view of the taste makers, you do not exist! The Charley Parker of Omaha may have just retired from music and got a job at the local Feed and Fuel, his genius sacrificed to the comfort of the known.

Atelier Fauré was Andrée's place. She ran it, did the design work and oversaw the studio's production. As I have mentioned, there was a large body of well trained people to bring Andrée's designs to life. These workers made minimum wage. This bit of information knocked me out! Minimum wage to produce these? From interviews with workers from the old studio, it is clear that Andrée was very well liked and ran the studio in a

Enameler at work at Fauré studio

familial way. The craftspeople at the studio all ate together and Andrée provided a light and comfortable atmosphere for the workers. Music and wine were also elements in the overall atmosphere of the studio.

The practice of assistants making the master's work is a very old tradition in the arts. You don't think Michelangelo painted the Sistine Chapel by himself, do you? Craftspeople of the time were trained to work under a master. This was not seen as demeaning: it was a job–it was your job–and probably better than being a door to door anvil salesman. This attitude is impossible today. The current fascination with fame and self-importance makes it nearly impossible for this type of studio situation to exist, at least in America.

R-L: Gérard Malabre; Andrée Fauré Malabre; Odette Lajudie, studio secretary; Mademoiselle Jarry, great artist, the first to paint landscapes with vitrifiable colors, specialist in Corot reproductions; Madame Vedrenne, specialist in florals on silver and an excellent salesperson; Lucie Dadat, specialist in Art Deco vases, forming a great team with M. Bardy; Suzanne Coiffe, specialist in portraits; M. Rozier, specialist in grisaille and also in Art Deco vases from 1950 on; M. Faure, the "cuiseur" of the studio who did all the firing of the enamel pieces.

For the workers of Atelier Fauré this was just a job, nothing extraordinary. At the height of production there were up to 25 workers in the studio.

The Fauré studio didn't have its own retail gallery until 1936. Before that, it was exclusively wholesale. The first fair they participated in was in 1931 in Lyon, and they continued to show their annual line of 60-100 pieces all through the war years. From these fairs they established clients in the USA, Australia, South America and all over Europe. There was one shop in Paris that handled the vases, called Damon and Delente, "Au Vase Etrusque", Place de la Madeleine. But the majority of the orders were taken at fairs and by Andrée's husband, Louis Malabre, a shoe salesman who took the Fauré line to

Early Fauré vases (private collection, France).

peddle along with his shoes. Louis Malabre is the unsung hero of the Fauré story. Louis was a good-natured salesman who took it upon himself to see that the Fauré work was everywhere. He and Andrée would get in their car and sell from Limoges through Spain and then take the ferry and continue in Morocco and Tangiers. Louis got the work out. Not quite as romantic as a boutique in Paris–more like a diner in St Paul–but efficient all the same.

This direct marketing is another reason why the studio never received its due. The art historians, collectors and museums were in Paris and larger contemporary cities. As I mentioned earlier, in many large cities there is a provincialism that doesn't allow for

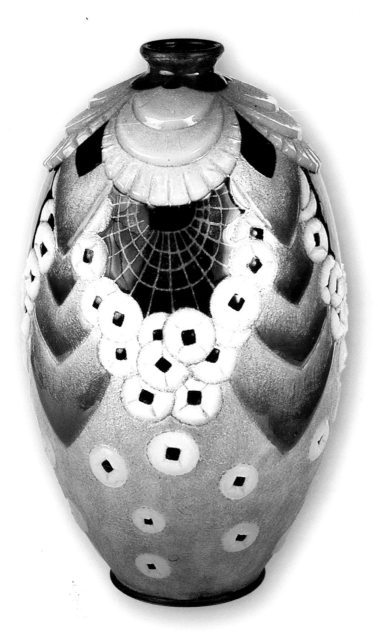

anything of value to happen outside the city's boundaries.

Camille's and Andrée's lack of ego in the enterprise also allowed the studio to drop from sight. Again, Camille's passion was hanging out in his country home with his cows.

It has taken over 80 years for the Fauré story to finally start being told.

Copper Forms and the Société Edmond Allain

There were 40 copper forms that the Fauré studio used as their canvases. In 1919 Camille Fauré established a relationship with the Edmond Allain Company of Paris. This company produced spun copper forms. (See Chapter 4 for a description of metal spinning.)

In the beginning Camille ordered forms that were already being produced by the Allain company, but when Andrée started working with the studio she began to design her own shapes.

She would do a line drawing with a scale specified. She gave each form a name based on a family member, pets included. The forms were also given a form number. These original drawings still exist and are kept in the archives of Edmond Allain Company in Paris.

All of the forms were designed between 1928 and 1929. Only one form ever had its name changed. Because of the war Adolphe was changed to Arthur.

Andrée would do watercolor drawings of each design. Fortunately several of these excellent and charming drawings still exist in a number of French collections.

Edmond Allain, founder of Société Allain, metal spinning and turning.

Street sign outside the Allain company at 14 rue Oberkampf in Paris.

Form for a "75" 35cm vase.

Original ledger with names, drawings and dimensions of the forms made by Société Allain for Atelier Fauré (they made all the forms used by Fauré from 1919 to the end of the studio's production).

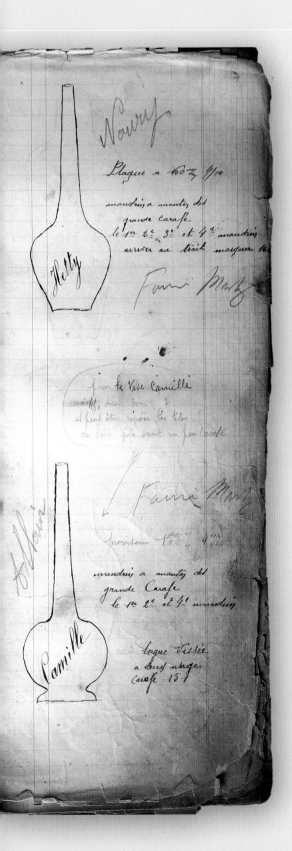

Bernard Vergne, grandson of Edmond Allain and current owner of Société Allain.

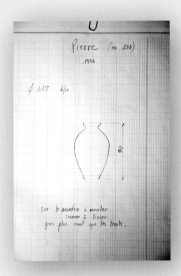

Page from ledger at Allain.

Copper form for a "Louis" vase, the largest vase made by Fauré.

Aluminum forms kept at Allain for reference.

Lampe Raquet bleue

Lilas rosé très clair

Bleu 2/3 avec
une pointe de cobalt bleu

fleurs blanches (opale vt) pétales séparés en jaune
et orange au centre
reliefs fond argent

§ 22 _ rouge
§ 22 bis bleu

rouge

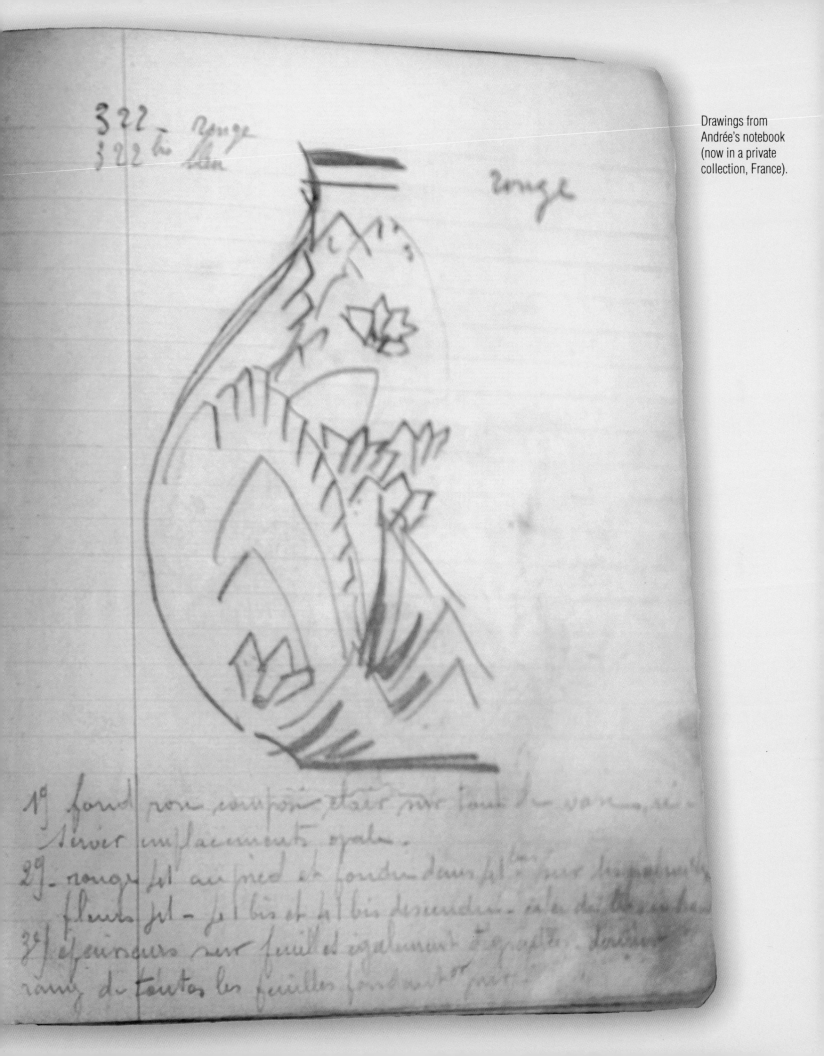

1° fond pour compose était sur tout de vernis, ses ...
servir emplacements opale.
2° rouge fut au pied et fondu dans fil à faire disparaître
fleurs fil - fil bis et de bis descendait- cela dit ...
3° éfaineurs sur feuil et également d'opale. ...
rang de toutes les feuilles fond dit-or ...

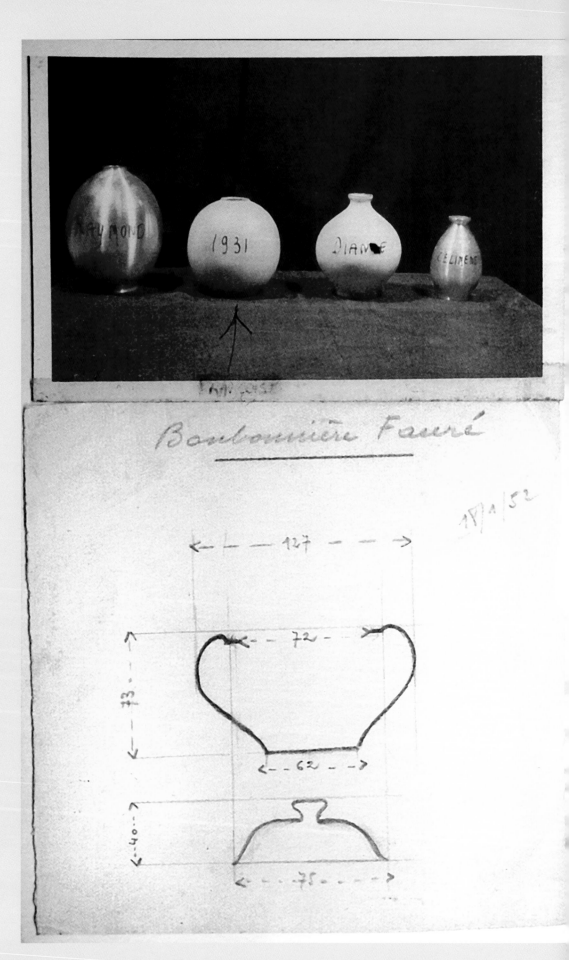

Old photos at the Allain
Company in Paris.

Unusual Fauré vase
(courtesy Rago Art
Center, New Jersey).

Assortment of Fauré vases.

From 1925 to 1950 the studio was very busy. They produced floral pieces, ashtrays, key and change holders, buttons, pins, jewelry, plaques with every imaginable motif, and the Art Deco designed pieces and new modernist designs done by Andrée and a few other designers. The employees were encouraged to design pieces if they so desired, but only a few ventured into the area of invention. You can see three or four distinct styles. You can also see some very bad designs! We do not know the percentage of pieces that were the sculpted pieces we associate with the studio. We know the number of copper forms that were produced from 1931 to 1994. We can guess at 1925 to 31. I would venture a guess that over the 75 year history of the studio about 12,000 pieces were

Variety of Fauré floral designs.

Fauré enamelled plaques
(Jones collection, Florida).

Fauré ring (Lucien
Geismar collection,
France).

made and, of those, 2,500 to 3,000 modern pieces were produced, the great majority of the work being the more conservative and traditional. Abstract art has always had a difficult time. The misguided desire of people wanting to know what it is limits the possibilities of what it can be. Realism is easy and comforting. Many of the Limoges enamelists recreated famous paintings as enamelled plaques. The florals were always the bread and butter of the studio. It is odd to see these pieces because they are so nonspecific. They are professional and attractive, but they aren't about to make a statement.

Throughout the history of the studio there would be the flights into contemporary art

Early Fauré vases (private collection, France. Left attributed to M. Bardy, design and execution.).

motifs beyond the Deco/modernist period, but it never met with the success of earlier times. Some very interesting work was produced post-war, showing the awareness of abstract expressionism and other trends that were happening in the art centers of the world, and these pieces should be looked at as serious works. The vases sold well up to 1950, but from 1950 to 1970 there was slow business in the Atelier Fauré.

Camille had passed away in 1955. Although Andrée had always run the shop, now it was official. Yet even with her father dead she never moved to take credit for her designs. Possibly this was simply a sound business decision.

In 1966 The Paris Museum of Decorative Arts did a show featuring the year 1925.

From this show the term "Art Deco" was coined. This showing sparked renewed interest in the Art Deco period and people started to look for studio Fauré work. The shop had been in the same location since 1936. The same tools, copper forms and enamels were used, and the original artist/designer was still in the studio. There were a few enamelists that still had the technique to create the distinctive vases. In response to this renewed interest the studio completed a number of the original designs from 30 years earlier, as well as producing larger numbers of new designs. (See Chapter 5.)

As discussed earlier, do not think for a moment that to produce one of these vases is a walk in the park. More like a walk in a minefield!

Starting in the late 1960's, a well-known Art Deco dealer from Paris established a relationship with Atelier Fauré. This must have been a Eureka moment for Mr. Lesieutre, the Parisian dealer.. He started to order a number of designs from Fauré. There were maybe 15 or so styles that he would order. These pieces were sold with a 1925 pedigree. Even though this is misrepresentation, I do not think these pieces should be thought of as reproductions or fakes. The work from this third phase of the studio is excellent! These pieces are the artists' work, made by the original designer, in the original studio in the same furnaces with the same tools and colors. (Chapter 5 has images of pieces from different periods for comparison.)

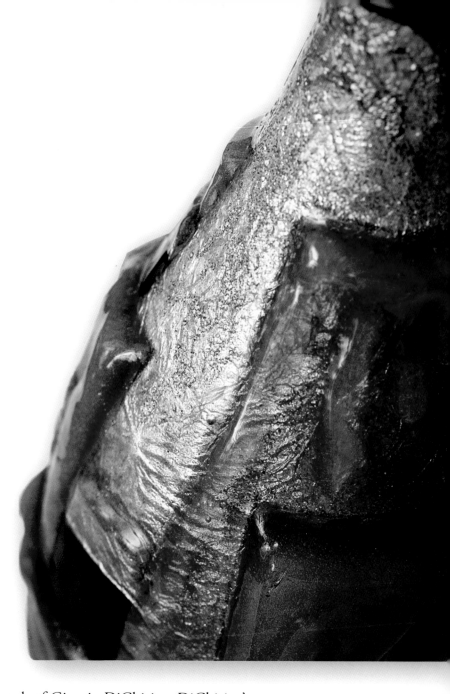

There is a historic case dealing with the work of Giorgio DiChirico. DiChirico's metaphysical paintings were very popular and collected broadly between 1910 and 1920. These brooding and melancholic cityscapes are now represented in most major modern museums throughout the world. After 1920, DiChirico left his metaphysical imagery and started a new series of pieces. After a number of years it became clear that these new pieces weren't as highly valued as his earlier, so DiChirico painted new metaphysical paintings and backdated them. He was brought to court for this practice, and his defense was that the date on the front of the painting was not a date but a number and part of the composition. He wasn't prosecuted, and no one really knows when many

DiChirico's were made. This in no way diminishes their value or importance. I believe the same is true of Fauré's work.

Andrée had a son, Gérard Malabre. He was a trained enamelist and, as a young man, he worked in the studio. He went on to become a pharmacist but never lost touch with the world of enameling. For a number of years he was even president of the local enamelers' guild. Andrée continued running the place into the early '80s. Her crew was small and orders had dropped off. Then a very large order of Deco style pieces and florals came in. The exact number and origin are unknown. Andrée now in her early 80s put on extra staff to fill the order. She completed and shipped the work but was never paid

Early Fauré vases (private collection, France).

for it. She was heartbroken. It wasn't possible for her to pay the extra staff. Because of this, Atelier Fauré went on the block. The business was sold to a Scandinavian woman who kept a number of Andrée's staff on. In a matter of 18 months the studio had been run into the ground. There was an auction of materials from the studio, but the business itself reverted to Andrée's son, Gérard. From this time on until his death in 1994 he would spend two days a week there with one technician, mostly doing repair work.

There are pieces of new designs that were made at this time that are easily recognizable. These pieces are not of as high a quality in either technique or design. The color palette is much different than in the earlier pieces, the whites are very different. Control of the

materials is so-so. This is important because in a good Fauré piece the handling of the
material can be breathtaking. The crisp edges and amazing knife work is not displayed
in these newest pieces. The color fades and blends are lacking, as is the transparency to
opaque transitions. But these are still interesting pieces and deserve to be considered
and collected, just not at the same price as the more refined and better designed.

The most telling thing is that there was an attempt at new designs. These designs are a
clumsy attempt to recreate the surface elements of the classic vases. These newer pieces
from 1985 to 1994, show no understanding of the original designs. Andrée understood
the fine art world and it informed her design work. This final phase of the studio is all

about decoration, not composition. The difficulty of the designs became obvious as clumsy pieces started to be produced.

The Atelier Fauré closed in 1994. The majority of the modernist pieces that are out in the world are from the original period of production, 1925 to 1950. A smaller number of pieces that were also very high quality were produced in the '60s and '70s, and finally the work of neo Faurés that went on until the end.

History holds a strong place for Fauré's work. I find the works especially appealing because of their fearless spirit.

It didn't simply use the avant-garde of the day for the creation of motifs. It innocently took the position of breaking down barriers and creating sculpture of great beauty, mystery and fun.

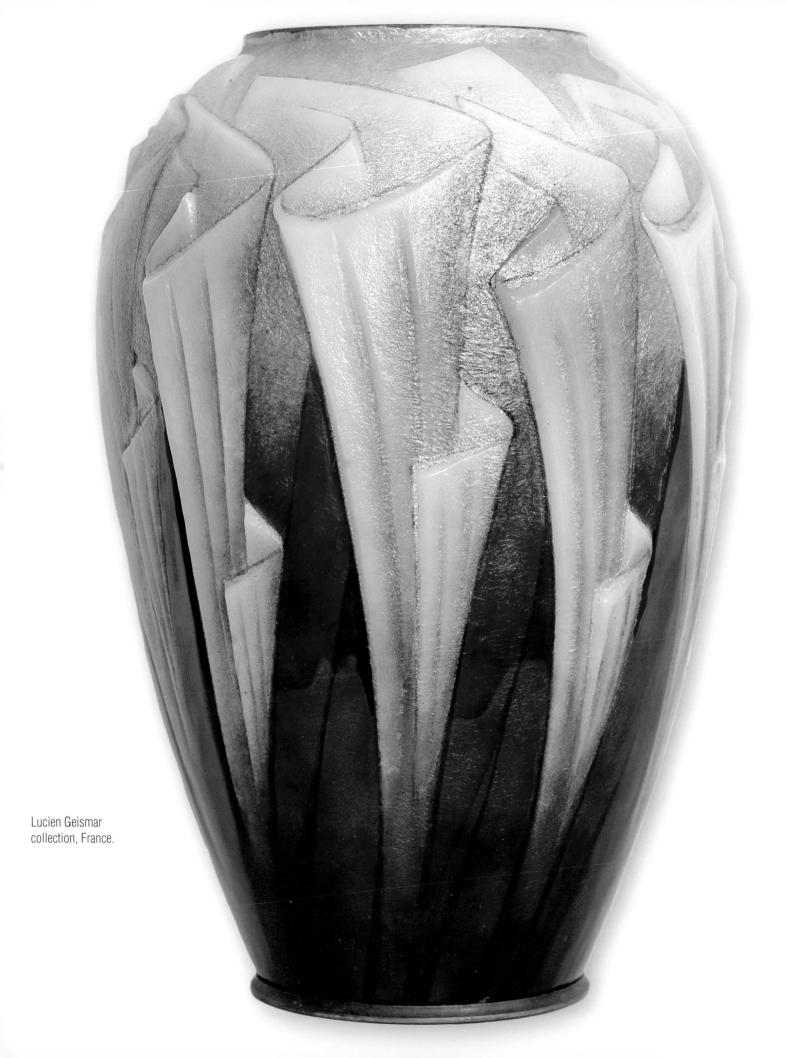

Lucien Geismar
collection, France.

The Making of a Vase

Andrée Fauré would pass the drawing for a vase on to one of the shop's masters. M. Martinot and M. Bardy were the specialists at translating and transferring the drawings. The master would take the flat art work, which may have been a 5" x 7" page out of a notebook, and create a detailed drawing that encompassed all sides of the vase. Andrée would discuss the design and confer on the colored enamels to be used. The next important consideration was how the colors should fade from transparent to translucent to opaque. The skill of the master cannot be understated. The pattern making problem of applying a flat design to a complex three dimensional object is applied geometry at work. Even more than that, the master would complete Andrée's ideas. These flat little color drawings were a general idea that the master would then have to complete in three dimensions. Many of the best pieces do not have repetitive themes, so two thirds of the vase was created by the master based on Andrée's theme. The masters were also allowed and encouraged to design their own work and a few of them did. Over time you can train your eye to recognize distinct features by specific designers.

The next consideration was the sculptural dimension of the surface. This is very important as it is the major defining attribute of a Fauré vase. The color transitions worked very beautifully with the built-up surfaces. By having the thinnest layers of the vase be the most transparent and luminous, it added to the dynamics of the built-up opaque edges and peaks. This final step would include the incised lines so unique to Fauré's work.

There are ways of getting the drawing onto the vase. There is the age-old technique with a twist. A very good way to transfer images is to use a pounce technique. You start by doing your drawing on a flat piece of butcher paper. You then use a hand tool that has a wheel with needle sharp points on it. You trace the pattern with the spiky wheel and it perforates the drawing.

Andrée's concept paintings..

Drawing clearly shows through enamel.

Transferring design to vase.

Dressmakers use this technique all the time, as do sign painters. The paintings on the Sistine Chapel ceiling could not have been drawn without this technique.

 The perforated drawing, in the hands of a master, is now applied to the copper vase and it is pounced with a chalk filled bag, The result is the drawing's outline has been transferred to the vessel.

At this point the chalk dot pattern is retraced with soft graphite, or painted with a liquid vitreous paint. The line withstands the firing and is frequently visible through transparent layers.

Drawing lines quite visible.

No visible drawing lines.

Another way of transferring the drawing was to divide the vase into radius sections. The vase would be placed on a piece of pattern paper that had a series of lines bisecting a circle. The vase was placed in the middle of the pattern. Then the master would extend the lines that the vase was resting on and bring the lines up onto the vase This is the same as applying a grid to a flat plane, but on a vase it is a bit trickier. A few of the masters could forgo the drawing transfer altogether and could work directly on the surface of the vessel. This is considered the height of mastery.

It took about 7-8 years to become a master, and the Fauré studio had up to 7 masters in the 25 person shop. To become a master was much more than simply a matter of time.

How the Copper Forms are Made–Metal Spinning

The Edmond Allain Company, introduced in the last chapter, has been in operation since 1910, and it is still in the family's hands, run by M. Bernard Vergne, grandson of the founder, Edmond Allain. This company produced all the copper forms for Fauré, Marty, Sarlandie and many other fine enamelers of the Deco period and beyond.

Metal spinning has been with us since the 10th century when the Chinese developed it. The process for spinning metal is simple and subtle. The basic concept is that a mold in the positive shape of the vase is spun on a lathe. An operator applying direct pressure to the spinning copper draws a circular copper plate over the spinning form.

So lets take it a step at a time.

The positive mold forms are made from hard wood (box elder a popular choice). There may be as many as 5 graduated forms to make one vase.

A circular copper plate is attached to the lathe. The shallowest wooden mold is attached in the center of the plate.

The lathe is spun at moderate speed. A wooden tool is applied to the edge of the spinning pizza of copper. The wooden tool is applied to the edge, which becomes rounded. The small rounded lip helps stabilize the form so it can be spun at high speed and not warp.

M. Bernard Vergne, owner of the Allain Company and grandson of founder, Edmond Allain, shows how the last wooden mold is removed in pieces from the finished copper form.

The wooden mold forms needed to spin the vase "Paule."

Metal spinner at the Allain company spinning a bronze disk.

Once the stabilizing lip is applied the lathe is brought to a higher speed.

The operator stands to the side of the spinning metal and braces a rubbing tool against stable pins. He then leverages his power against the spinning form and attempts to draw the metal over the form.

The operator needs to be able to sense the structure of the metal in order to prevent it from fatiguing. If you have ever taken a piece of wire and bent it back and forth for a while, you will notice that at a certain point the resistance of the metal will relax and within another bend or two the wire separates: this is metal fatigue. The molecules in the metal line up in straight lines. If you bend the metal too much the straight lines of molecules act like the perforation on a sheet of stamps. It is fine for the stamps to separate along the perforated lines, but not for the metal.

To stop this from happening to the copper spinnings they must be tempered. Tempering is simply heating the copper up with a large rosette torch. This simple process realigns the metal and allows it to continue being formed. This process is now repeated with each additional mold section until the final draw. At this point it is necessary to use a sectioned positive mold. Because the vases have a top and bottom smaller than the mold form, it is necessary for the form to come apart in pieces and be removed one piece at a time.

A complicated form such as the one pictured would take 4 to 5 hours to complete.

Everything about the Fauré process is difficult.

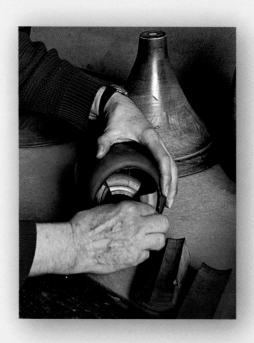

Fauré studio.

To elevate this delicate craft to a higher plateau it took an intangible skill that no matter how long you worked at it would never be attainable through simple practice. If all it took was practice to become a master at anything, we would have a lot of Yo-Yo Mas and Tiger Woods around. At this moment in time there are no masters left that can recreate the sharp-edged, sculpted Fauré vases of the Art Deco period. A few people can get close but not so close.

The relationship of master and apprentice was very good. The young workers respected the older masters and visa versa. The masters would pick an apprentice to pass their techniques and some secrets on to. Without this focused attention, it was not possible

Fauré signature piece (Lucien Geismar collection, France).

to gain all of the information necessary to master the Fauré technique. It is the masters that worked on the dimensional Deco and Modernist pieces. Unlike the florals that were doable by any of the workers in the shop, only the masters produced the signature work. The masters never passed all of their techniques onto the apprentices. They were always left with a bit undone. This was a genteel way of protecting one's job, and like the 5¢ candy, they have become extinct. No one can make these pieces today!

The process to create one vase includes several additional, laborious and delicate steps. Enamel is basically a very finely ground glass that is mixed with specific metal oxides. The glass and the oxides are melted to a liquid state. At a specific temperature a small

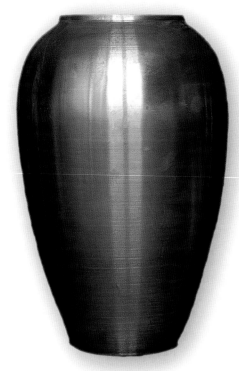

Copper vase form
(Société Allain, Paris).

Fauré enamel palettes and original Fauré colors bought by Paul Buforn, a former Fauré employee, when the shop was sold. This quality of enamel color has become extinct as mass production methods took over from the former manual production.

ladle (about half a pint) is dipped into the molten material and then poured on a marver (one-inch-thick smooth steel table). The glass forms a puddle and quickly cools and hardens. In a minute or so a worker will toss many hardened puddles of the same color into a bin. The individual pizza-sized puddles shatter and are then ground to powders of different fineness. It is this powder that will be applied to the copper vessels.

Copper is used for the forms because it has the same expansion coefficient as glass. This allows the copper and the glass to expand and contract at the same rate and not stress the glass. Stressing translates to cracks, fractures and the glass actually popping off.

Next the interior and exterior are coated with a transparent layer of clear enamel. This is

Applying silver foil to the form.

Effect of the silver foil.

Occasionally gold foil was used instead of silver.

a very critical step, as it will help stabilize the vases against thermal shock in the numerous trips in and out of the furnace. Next a layer of silver foil is applied to the exterior of the vase with a water-based glue very similar to wallpaper paste. Before the foil is applied, it is whacked several times with a stiff wire brush. This perforates the silver and tempers it, making it easier to apply and creating better adhesion. The silver foil is what gives the vases their incredible luminosity. Light will pass through the various layers of enamel, hit the silver and reflect color and light through the layers. An important point about the silver is that when the piece was completed, air could not be allowed to come in contact with the silver. If it did, the silver would tarnish and dark streaks or patches

Enameler at the Atelier Fauré in the early days, working on a floral vase.

would appear. The pounce pattern or vertical lines are applied at this point.

The enamel colors have slightly different working temperatures: dark and hot colors are softer and melt faster; the cool colors are stiff and melt a little hotter. Keep this in mind as you continue to follow this process.

At this point the craftsman takes a long stick and puts it through the bottom of the vase (which is open at this time) and out the top. This will allow the vase to be supported and turned without any of its sides being touched. The enamels, which have a fine mud like consistency, are placed in numerous cups directly in front of the craftsman. The grit size of the enamels is important: the finer the grit the more detail you can achieve.

Mauricette Pinoteau who worked with Andrée Fauré in the 1970's and now has her own studio and shop in Limoges, demonstrates how the enamel is built up and patterned.

If you are doing a portrait on a plaque and you want fine detail for eyes, hair, etc., you would use very fine grit. For the sculptural Fauré vases a very large, sandy grit was used. Now with a small, rigid, spatula-like tool the moist, sandy enamel is applied. This is very much like building a sand castle. You lay down some of the enamel and delicately tamp it down. Remember building sand castles? To get any scale out of them you must have the proper mixture of water and sand so you can compact the sand to give it structure. It is exactly the same with the Fauré vases, except your sand castle is on a circular surface that is balanced on a stick. When one layer is completed, paper towels are gently applied to the surface to absorb moisture from that layer. Then another layer is applied.

The successful designs were often repeated with some variation (private collection, Paris).

This is a very delicate process that takes an uncompromising eye and hand. The layer that is applied on the silver is usually transparent and it follows the drawing that is on the vase. This layer is flat and carries the background colors.

During this process it was possible for Andrée to see the development of the individual pieces and adjustments could be made at this time. Andrée was very gentle and diplomatic. If she saw a piece that was not progressing properly she would spirit it away, give it to another worker to make it right and give the original worker a replacement job. Andrée was very particular about what left the shop with the family name on it.

The next step is building up the enamel, including the sculpting of the elevated surface.

Award winning lamp and matching vase (vase Jones collection, Florida and same vase is in the Museum of Decorative Arts, Paris).

After a number of firings and building up the surfaces, the angular ridges or smooth rounded edges were additionally sculpted into the unfired enamels. Think about all of this as you look at the complex designs.

So we have a vase from 3" to 15" tall. It is supported on a stick in front of the craftsperson. They apply numerous layers of a sandy mud-like material to the vase, being careful not to damage this unstable surface. This process could take from a day to weeks. The vases were then allowed to dry before the final step of firing.

The furnace was originally coal fired and ran at 1653° Fahrenheit (1000° Centigrade).

The original, charcoal burning Fauré kiln.

Pitting caused by firing in the charcoal kiln.

After the war the furnace was converted to electric. The pieces that were fired in the coal furnace have carbon deposits and minor pitting on the interior enamel of the vases. This is a good way to judge the age of a piece.

Let's recap: we have a copper vessel that is fired with an inner and outer layer of enamel; then silver foil is applied; then the design is drawn or painted onto the foil; then the moist enamel powders are applied and tamped down in successive layers; finally a series of flash firings take place, and, through intuitive skill, these impossible objects are brought into existence.

The enamel is lead glass based. Neon tubes are also lead glass. This type of glass is very

Vase inside electric kiln which was introduced after WW II.

forgiving and soft (low melting point), and it allows for heat to be brought directly into contact with the glass and not have it fracture.

The vases have been going through a series of flash firings. This means that the piece is put into the hot furnace for a very short time (not more than 5 minutes), usually measured by the color of the vessel being fired rather than time or temperature. The idea is to get the enamel to vitrify. (Vitrification is the process of all of the grit becoming one without distorting. Stoneware is vitrified. If you flick a piece of stoneware it will ring. That resonance is a sign of vitrification). The vase is removed from the furnace to prevent overheating. If the piece is left in too long it will melt and sag, losing its definition. An-

A good example of the very best of Fauré techniques.

other trick to assure the surface stays where you want it to is to alternate firing right side up and then upside down. This allows heat and gravity to work together. The vase will make a minimum of 15 and a maximum of 25 trips into the furnace. After 25 firings the silver foil will lose its integrity. This flash firing technique along with the enamel application was developed by Alexandre Marty.

We do not know who developed the most exotic of all techniques – the sharp built up edges. When we visited Mauricette Pinoteau (who worked with Andrée Fauré), she was astonished by photos showing the quality and craftsmanship of the early pieces, which were beyond the skill of anyone practicing in her day. The edges were applied as a

second-to-last operation. After the vase had been just about completed, a master would take the vase and with a wet copper wheel (traditional cutting tool for cut glass), incise lines in raised glass/enamel surfaces. The design concept had to be in mind long before the artist arrived at this point.

Once the cutting had been done the piece would be fired one last time. This time it was for a shorter time and at lower heat. The hard ground edges were heated to the point of just starting to soften and then the vase was removed from the furnace. The edges are softened slightly, but the definition is unmistakable. The pieces that have this work are the rarest of all the Fauré vases.

There were a good number of failed vases, if for no other reason than the simple fact that a piece needs to physically be brought in and out of the hot furnace at least 15 times. The process is exacting and intuitive at the same time. The furnace man had to be able to judge heat based on the color of the vessel in the fire. Experience and touch is what made for magic in the flames.

Lucien Geismar
collection, France.

Useful Fauré Stuff

At the time of this writing, Art Deco and Modernist Fauré enamels are ragarded as the ugly country cousins by the Parisian and other world art centers. This can be a very good thing for the person that wants to collect or to simply observe what may happen in the next couple of years to this underappreciated artwork. Many people who are recent converts to the world of Art Deco and Modernist design will get the rare opportunity to see undiscovered masterpieces enter the marketplace and the museum collections.

I intend for the remainder of this book to help in giving language to the process of a deeper appreciation. Yes these things are pretty but the good ones have more to them than a surface.

The other thing that I touch on is the field of collecting. With Fauré there are a few hints that can go a long way to help sort out new from old, good from poor, and rare from common.

Jones collection, Florida

113

Five views of one vase

I have chosen this vase because of its complexity and energy. When I first saw this piece I was photographing Bill Jones' collection. It didn't strike me immediately; there were many other pieces that demanded immediate attention. This vase was on a shelf above eye level. I was looking at the piece from below and noticed what visually felt like tiles set in grout. I picked the piece up and had a WOW moment. The composition was complex and dense but not chaotic. I thought about glass origami, Charlie Parker solos, Schoenberg compositions, what it was like to experience the premiere of the Rights of Spring or to be at the Armory show.

Please excuse my ability to be deeply moved, but I was.

The section that looks like tiles is composed of globular two-tone blue forms suspended in a grey field. The two blues have a defined pattern that continues from piece to piece and across the grey field. I didn't see this subtlety on first view. The globs have a liquid feel; they perceptually refer to several blue puddles. But on further investigation these puddles have internal sections of a second color whose form continues over the space of the grey grout-like background. They could have been a solid design element that has melted and is now drifting apart. This compositional element establishes a flowing background that is similar to flowing water under an ice sheet or the molten magma that is at the core of our own planet.

This type of visual reference is common to art criticism; what makes it useful is that all of the references are common knowledge and that collective body of information allows us to be moved by what we experience.

Continuing on, you have the angular forms that create a visual (crust) layer above the globular forms. These larger angular forms remind me of the tonal clusters of dissonant orchestral music. The large forms in blue and black move you around the form until you encounter clusters of opal that burst like fireworks or flower blossoms. And finally a series of double saw tooth angles chew and fold onto the foreground. These particular forms are very representative of the Futurist paintings of Fortunato Depero.

There are a number of variations on this theme but none reach the inspired and absurd heights of this piece in the Jones collection. I think it is safe to say that these pieces were designed and fabricated by one designer. If this piece had been done in the psychedelic 1960s, I would have known how it was inspired. But in 1930s Limoges, it is quite a different proposition.

You may prefer other forms. but take a moment to study this as a statement of how fearless and accomplished the studio was.

Jones collection, Florida, attributed to M. Rozier, design and execution..

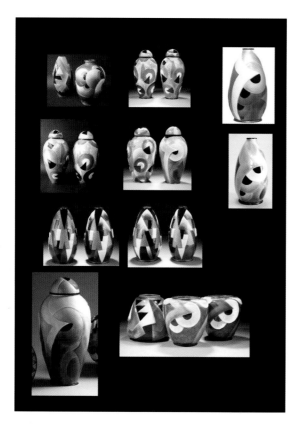

Late Fauré vases (various private collections, UK and USA).

Lucien Geismar collection, France.

Collecting

If you get interested in collecting Fauré pieces, I have a few recommendations.

If you are willing to look, they do come up. Many were sold in North and South America, France and other parts of Europe in 2005. I am aware of 12 pieces that came up that were trackable online. I am sure there must have been more, plus all of the pieces that traded privately.

Out of these 12 there was one excellent museum quality piece (USA). This piece was extraordinary and sold for $14,500. Pieces of this quality are extremely rare and will bring high prices.

Jones collection, Florida.

Late Fauré vases, (private collections Australia, UK and USA).

Private collection, London.

Jones collection, Florida.

A second piece that was very good is an original model that has been duplicated many times in the phase two and three periods (see pages 137-141). In 2005, four of these pattern phase-three pieces were available (England). They were in the $2,000 to $2,500 range. The phase one pieces went for $10,000 (USA). There was another excellent and unusual example that went for a bargain price of $2,400 (USA). This one, the checked pattern, is very cool and should appeal to anyone who was a fan of two-tone ska music and now collects Art Deco (we do grow up). And then one more phase two piece that was very good came from the estate of Elton John and sold for $4,800 (Australia). Fve more pieces of phase three pedigree went for about

Late Fauré vases (various private collections).

Sonnabend collection. Purchased in 1970 directly from Andrée Malabre as part of a collection of 22 pieces.

$2,000 to $3,500 (England and USA).

Because of the records I have from the Edmond Allain Company, I have a good idea of the number of copper forms that were made between 1931 and 1994. We can guess at the 5 year period of 1925 to 1930. (See pages 130-1 for the total numbers of forms.)

There were probably 2500 to 3000 Art Deco/Modernist vases made during the history of the atelier. Of those, half are top quality and I believe a number of these pieces are unique. Even though edition numbers are suggested on the drawings, I feel very strongly that if a style sold well, they would sell as many as they could. Some of the pieces that didn't sell well became unique examples. Because the Deco pieces were so difficult to make they never made more

Three fiddlehead fern pattern vases (two large, one small). (Lucien Geismar collection, France [above], private collection, France [right], Jones collection, Florida, [below right].Note: there is also a third large matching vase in the Victoria & Albert Museum, London.Vases attributed to M. Bardy team, 1945-55.)

than one at a time and would not produce a second until the first was bought and paid for. Each of the duplicates was made by the original artist: this was the only way to control the duplication. To see two or more of the same designs together is amazing. They were able to accurately duplicate their work through pure skill and talent.

All three vases, private collection, France.

Private collection, France
(above and right).

Lucien Geismar collection, France.

Jones collection, Florida.

Vases from three different collections: private collection, France; Lucien Geismar collection, France; Jones collection, Florida.

Private collection, France.

Jones collection, Florida.

Maison Gerard, New York.

Sonnabend collection, New York.

Private collection, France.   Lucien Geismar collection, France.

Private collection, France.

Two views of one vase, (private
collection, France).

Two views of one vase, (private
collection, France).

How many vases *did* Fauré produce and when?

The Big Picture

The Edmond Allain Company made all of the copper forms used by the Atelier Fauré. They also kept very good records of the vases made and delivered to Fauré. Unfortunately the records begin in 1931. It's possible that the first line on the graph on this page represents the production up until

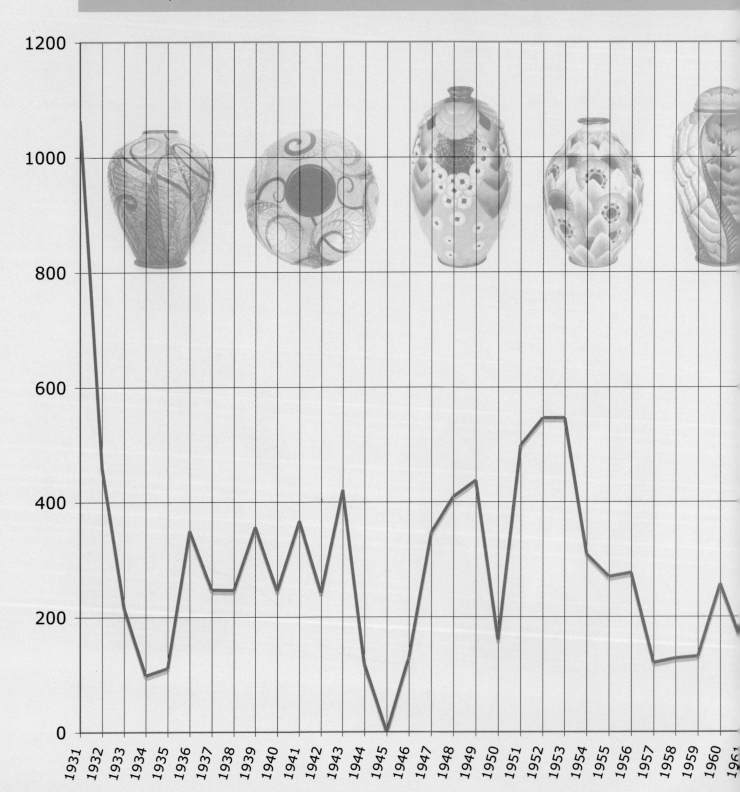

1931, as the figure for 1931 is very high. This is not clear in the records.

This chart is a fairly accurate depiction of the data in the Allain records. There may be some very minor inaccuracies, but the overall picture is as shown and the totals are fairly accurate.

Names and numbers of some of the popular vase forms.

Name Approx. Height	Form	Drawing	Example	Approximate number made
Jacques or Jack 11cm/4.5"				**833**
Célimène 11.5cm/4.5"				**602**
Gros Monitz 11cm/4.5"				**595**
Hoock 14cm/5.5"				**443**
Raymond 17cm/6.75"				**428**

Name Approx. Height	Form	Drawing	Example	Approximate number made
Jeanne 13cm/5″				**363**
Léon 11cm/4.5″				**352**
Louis 17cm/5″				**351**
Marcel 23cm/9″				**327**
Diane 14cm/5.5″				**325**

Name Approx. Height	Form	Drawing	Example	Approximate number made
Adolphe/ Arthur 28cm/10.5″				**281**
Primerose 30cm/12″				**280**
Antonio 27cm/11.25″				**244**
1931 14cm/5.5″				**234**
Suzon 15cm/6″				**207**

Name Approx. Height	Form	Drawing	Example	Approximate number made
Vincent 15cm/6″				**207**
Yvonne 12cm/4.75″				**203**
Azyadée I 30cm/12″				**194**
Lucien 30cm/12″				**184**
75/30 30cm/12″				**179**

Name Approx. Height	Form	Drawing	Example	Approximate number made
Mathias 25cm/10″				173
René 30cm/12″				153
Emile 19.5cm/7.75″				124
Gérard 9cm/3.5″				116
Marie-Paule 18cm/7″				96

Four Phases of Fauré

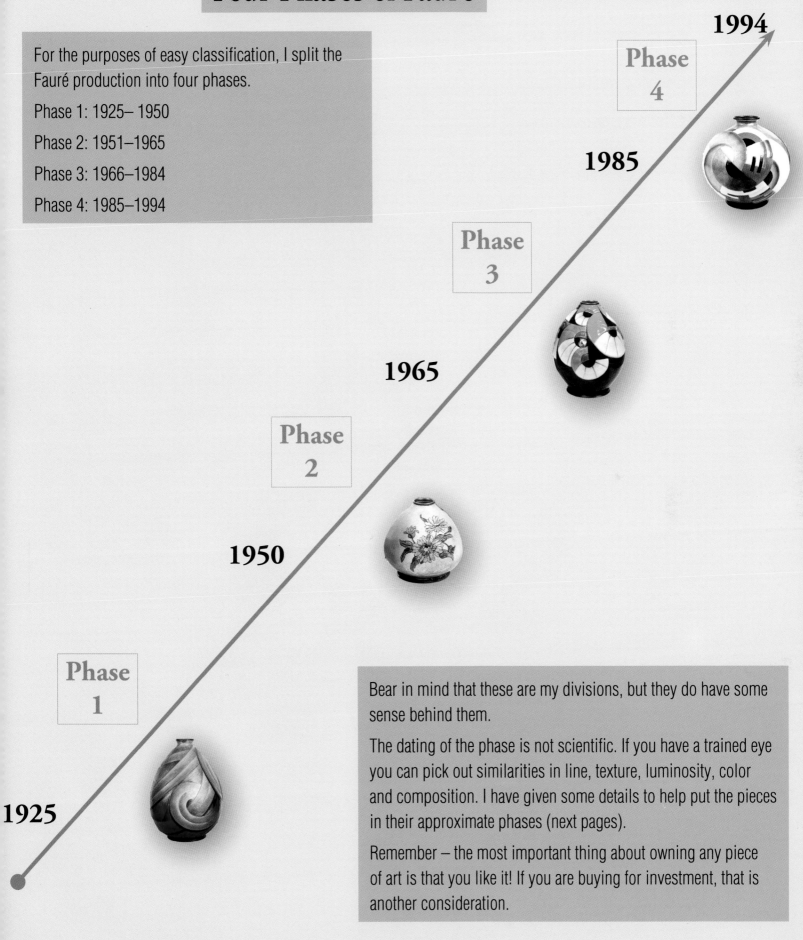

For the purposes of easy classification, I split the Fauré production into four phases.

Phase 1: 1925– 1950

Phase 2: 1951–1965

Phase 3: 1966–1984

Phase 4: 1985–1994

1994

Phase 4

1985

Phase 3

1965

Phase 2

1950

Phase 1

1925

Bear in mind that these are my divisions, but they do have some sense behind them.

The dating of the phase is not scientific. If you have a trained eye you can pick out similarities in line, texture, luminosity, color and composition. I have given some details to help put the pieces in their approximate phases (next pages).

Remember – the most important thing about owning any piece of art is that you like it! If you are buying for investment, that is another consideration.

Phase 1

Phase one has the benefit of excitement and discovery. It is true that the best artisans also worked between 1925 and 1950, but what can't be overstated is the excitement of the time. Making art in France while the art world was exploding with innovation and adventure is the best possible scenario for great things to be done.

Color dynamism, extreme technique and daring design mark this first phase. This piece (right) is one of the earliest pieces represented here. I would place it between 1925 and 1929. In addition to having a flat bottom, this piece has the most classic of all Deco designs. If you have any Deco references you will find this leaf pattern in glass vases, Edgar Brandt's iron work, architectural detail, textile designs and graphic materials.

The other examples represented feature the highest degree of technical finesse and great composition.

The color palettes of the day were also used.

Phase 2

This period is marked by many floral designs that aren't really that distinguishable from other periods. There are also the plaques, ashtrays, jewelry etc. This was a period of simply keeping the place open and everyone working. I feel sure that some abstract pieces were made during this time and, if we are lucky, the next book to be written about Fauré will have found or purchased the sales records of the company and be able to better identify this low point in the studio's history.

Phase 3.

Here we see the effect of the rediscovery of Art Deco and the involvement of Parisian art dealer Alain Lesieutre. There were many patterns that were duplicated during this phase. This isn't a bad thing, this allows for more reasonable prices of pieces that are known to be the most easily found. The quality issues are very important in this period. Because there were many good people from the original studio still working at the beginning of this phase, the quality of their pieces is excellent. But as time moved on, some of the quality slipped. Do not discount this period: some great stuff came out of it.

Phase 4

This is after the company was sold and Andrée had passed away. Several new pieces were designed, but they do not come up to the design standard of the studio. The quality of craftsmanship has seriously dropped off and the enamels themselves seemed to be inferior.

The last brochure of the Atelier Fauré showing the last pieces produced.

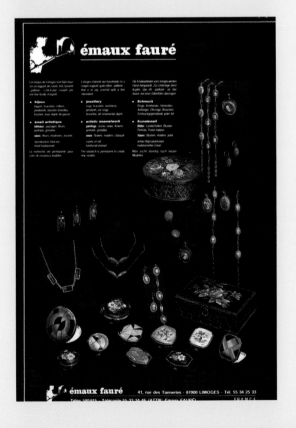

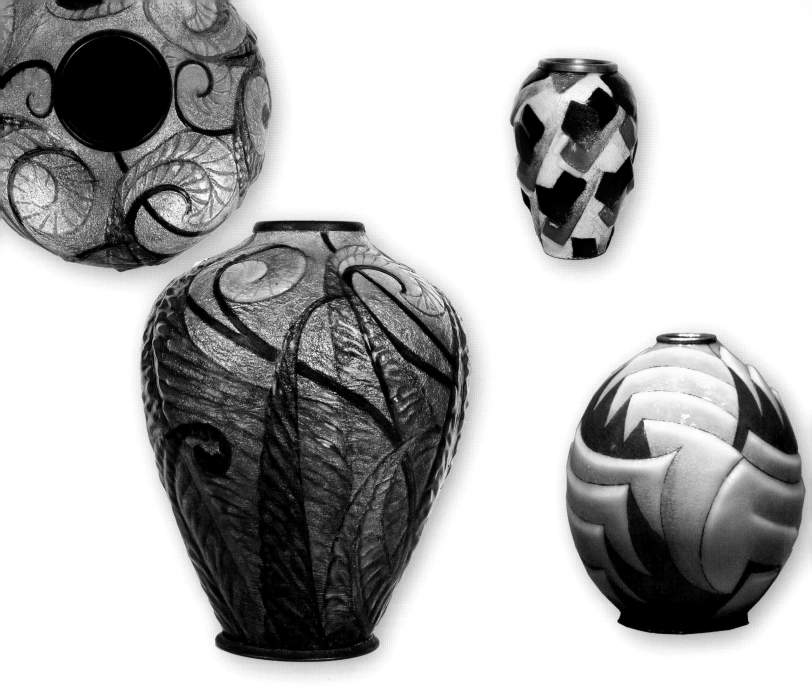

My experience in the world of art has shown me that the best pieces are usually not the most popular. So I do think there are a fair number of unique pieces out there. The Art Deco pieces are the most difficult and expensive of all the work ever to come out of the studio. The florals, figurative pieces, and plaques would make up about 85% of the Fauré output. These pieces are the easiest to find and not expensive at this writing. eBay seems to frequently have plaques, florals and occasionally figurative pieces on offer. A few times a year high quality pieces will also find their way through an eBay auction site. The Art Deco vases were always expensive and consequently were taken care of. The chances of finding one at the Goodwill store aren't real high! But you never know: as more people get interested, more pieces will

emerge. The smell of money always sharpens dealers' vision and pieces of quality in different states of repair will enter the market. No one can repair the sharp edged pieces today; these pieces are best left as-is. Soft edged pieces can possibly be repaired by one or two enamelers still practicing. Repairing them properly means re-firing the entire piece and matching the enamels. I am sure that there are restorers who can approximate the look with epoxies, but I don't recommend it. The vases are very strong and can take some abuse, so if you find a very good piece but it has some minor damage I would recommend getting it. Florals, figuratives and plaques should be in near perfect condition. They are not hard to find.

Some of the drawings done by Andrée are dated. This can tell you when the design originated

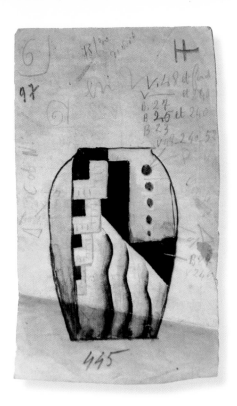

and at least one piece was made. If subsequent pieces were made we wouldn't know the date, but I think it would be closer to the dated drawing than not.

The drawings themselves are very collectible and difficult to find. The Paris Museum of Decorative Arts has 18 of the drawings in their collection along with a couple of vases.

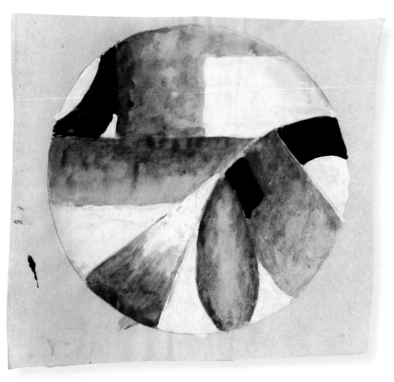

The next piece of information is a step above well-founded rumor. I have been trying to verify it, but a lot of time has slipped by and many of the questions are of little importance to the people who would know the answers.

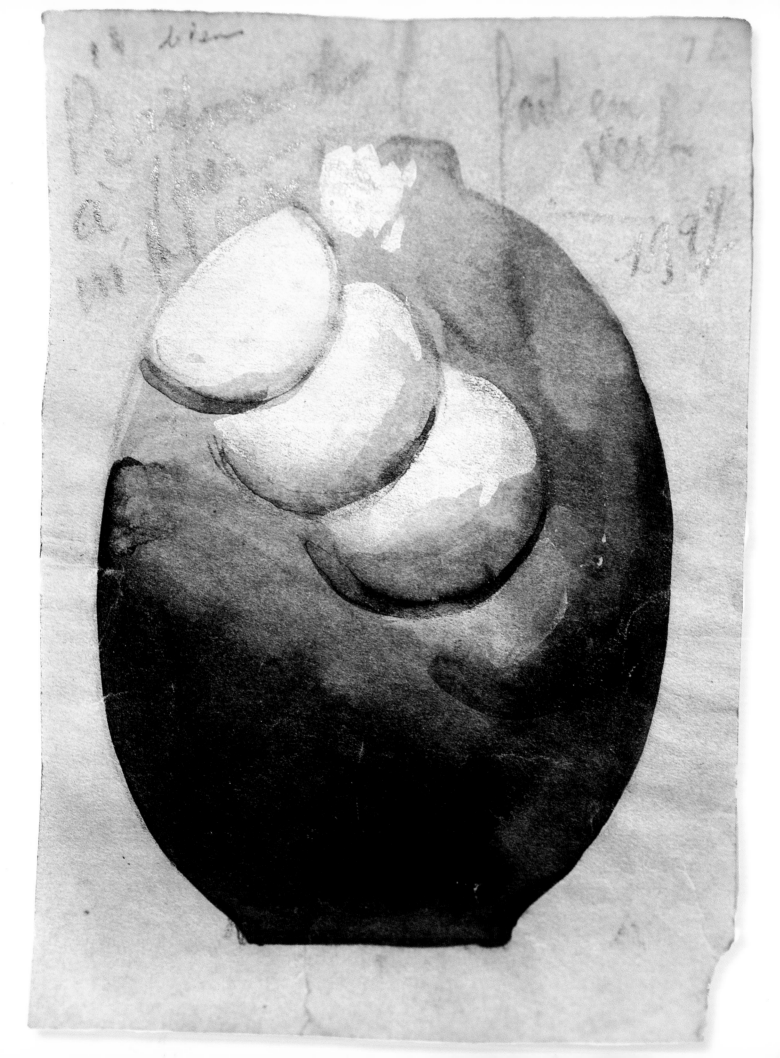

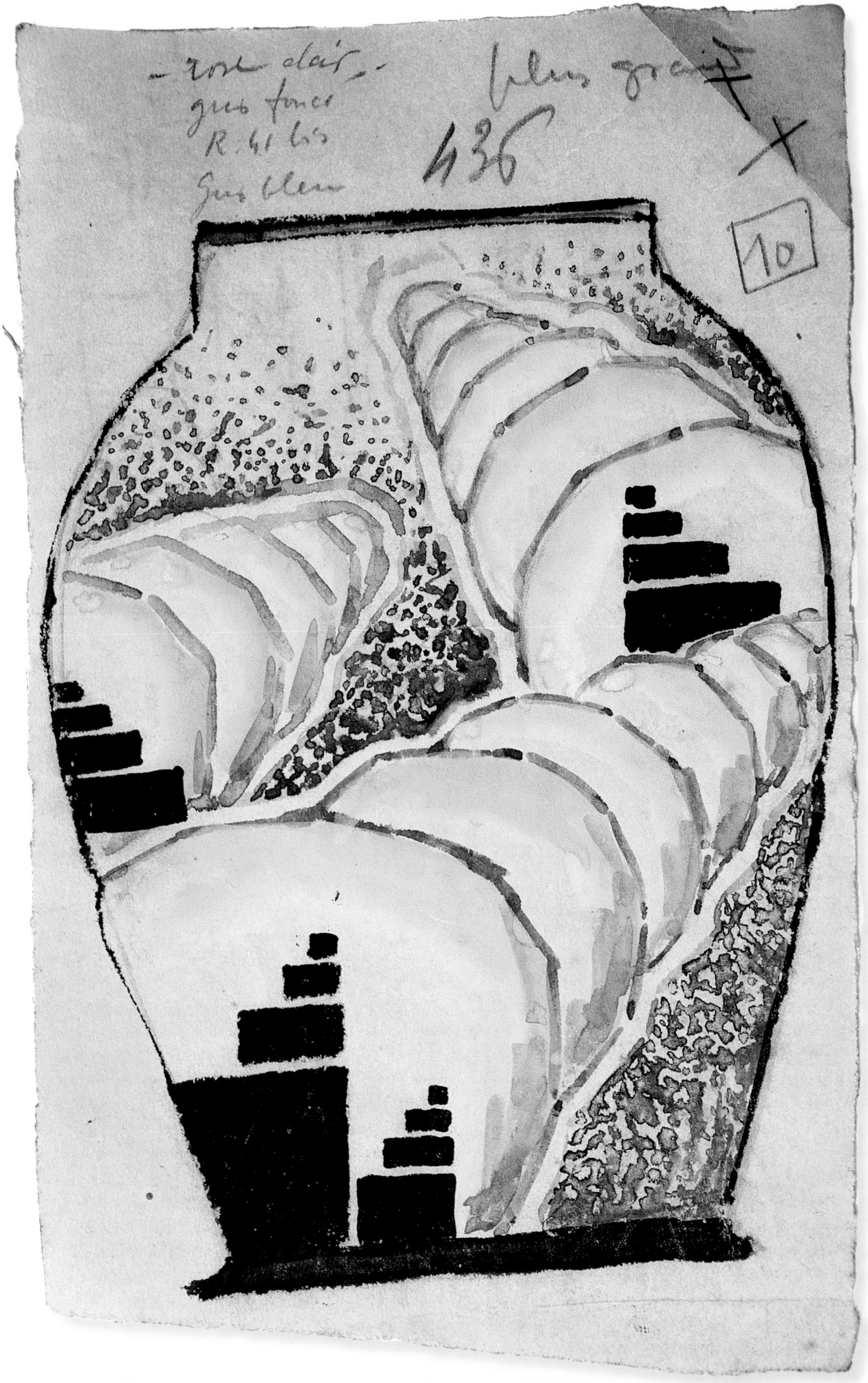

- rose clair -
gris foncé
R. 41 bis
gris bleu

bleus gris

436

10

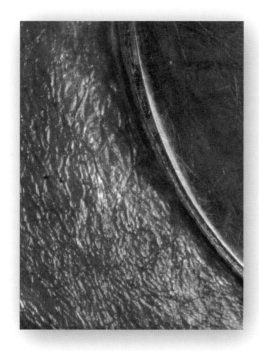

Dating

The spinning process requires that the bottom of the vases are left open. This is to extract the mold. This makes it necessary to somehow close the bottom of the vessel. There are two distinct bottoms. Some Art Deco dealers of note have stated that the way to tell if your piece is from the original period is to check for a flat bottom. The flat bottom is actually a piece of flat metal that is punched to the size of the hole in the bottom of the vase. This flat metal plate fits flush into the bottom of the vase. I have only found these bottoms on obviously older pieces. You can tell they are older because they are technically beyond what the later practitioners could handle. The sharp edges are key to identifying the early pieces. Match the

sharp edges with complexity and you most certainly can spot a first period piece. During the early '70s there were a few skilled workers still available that could handle the sharp edges on a minor scale, but nowhere near the way the earlier masters could.

The term "flat" equates to a marble counter top or an inch thick plate of steel.

The other bottom is spun. These spun bottoms weren't made by Edmond Allain until 1931. After '31 the spun bottoms and lips were in use. You can see the lines from the spinning (like a record album) and they have a lip that comes up and over the exterior of the piece so the vase actually sits in it. The bottom is also not flat. Take an UNOPENED quart pickle jar or other jar of some size that has a wide mouth. Feel the top of the jar. The internal vacuum in

Private collection, Paris,
attributed to M. Bardy,
design and execution.

the jar creates a very minor depression. This is not a truly flat surface. This depression and small lip that raises around the bottom is the spun base. The minor deflection between the two is possibly a way to assess the age of the pieces.

One additional clue is that the earlier pieces were also fired in a coal furnace, and the carbon pits the enamel on the interiors of these pieces (see page 102).

The fact of the matter is: a really good piece is a really good piece. Your best tool is your eye.

The extremely difficult pieces with great color fades, sharp edges and dimensional build-up are stunning no matter when they were made.

The examples shown are a good indication of what to look for.

The most important thing is to buy what you like. There is no reason to buy an IMPOR-TANT piece that you don't like. Life is too short. Go for what you like.

Various covered vases from different time periods.

Then there were lamps!

Structure of a master work.

Slight pebbly texture is left from the last firing that isn't allowed to melt completely. This firing also polishes the wheel cut grooves.

Hard edged grooves are wheel cut and flame polished in the last firing. This work wasn't done past 1950.

Base coat is applied directly over the silver foil. This establishes a transparent base and carries the vases design.

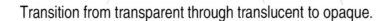

Transition from transparent through translucent to opaque.

The use of color, quality of the composition and mastery of the material put this piece in the highest level of achievement to come out of Atelier Fauré.

Deconstruction of an '80s vase.

Lack of line control
The curves do not flow
in a continuous arc.

Whites are dull and lack luminosity
they have an applied lard quality.

Compromised skill
creates weak attempt
at classic Faure pattern.

Fuzzy details and no
articulated line work.

Lucien Geismar collection, France..

Doodle

I have spent hours looking at this vase. It may tie for the vase with the most going on!

This particular vase casually shows craftsmanship of the highest level in the lightest possible way. The composition has the structure of a doodle on a note pad next to your phone. There are some squiggly lines, some floral flourishes, a checked treatment, a couple of dots, paisley and a flying moustache all together. This is a neat trick to pull off, and it is a nearly impossible thing to do in enamel. This vase is a solo of relaxed expertise that frolics instead of intimidates. In contemporary terms, I think of Frank Stella's large active and colorful wall pieces as counterparts to this particular Fauré vase.

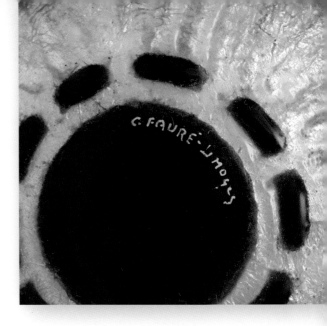

All the Fauré pieces were signed with the studio name, never with the name of the individual artists.

Rago Art Center, New Jersey.

Jones collection, Florida.

Jones collection, Florida.

Jones collection, Florida.

From Lesieutre collection, current
whereabouts, unknown.

Jones collection, Florida (a vase matching the vase on the
right is also in the Museum of Decorative Arts, Paris).

Sonnabend collection,
New York City.

Private collection, Paris.

Lucien Geismar collection, France.

Sonnabend collection,
New York City.

Jones collection, Florida..

Envoi

There are moments when time and circumstances coalesce to produce something that is so pure and true that by the time its original energy has been exhausted it has spawned a second generation. With each succeeding generation the purity is lost, and frequently the original gesture is forgotten or bent to fit a convenient story line.

Blues and rock n' roll music are perfect examples of a moment that seeped out of postwar America. This simple music spoke a new language to a young audience that had never had a voice before. This exuberant and innocent sound lasted about 10 years before the financial potential of the music overpowered the music itself. This is the nature of success.

The story of Atelier Fauré is similar to Sun Records. Instead of Elvis walking in to make a record for his mom's birthday, Andrée Fauré was given creative control of her father's enamel studio. The power of art moved her in very true directions. Just like bebop magically developing at Minton's Playhouse in Harlem, Andrée Fauré made art that would outlast the critics who are now forgotten.

Studio Fauré did not build on the past: it created a moment that would be unique to the point that it could not be copied.

The finest pieces of Fauré work rival any of the Art Deco masters and outdo them on the grounds of bold originality, fearless experimentation and an integration of the modern art of its day.

Thank you!

I would like to thank the numerous people who so graciously gave of their time and information to make this book possible.

I must first thank all of the anonymous contributors who risked retribution or other unspoken threats, one in particular who went way above and beyond in providing assistance.

David Ryan for being my cheering section and always pushing me onwards. Anne Ryan for giving me confidence in my unorthodox research methods.

To Bill and Jan Jones for sharing their wonderful collection and home with me.

To Lucien Geismar for sharing his collection and abundant knowledge.

To the anonymous mystery Parisian collector for sharing his stunning collection of Fauré vases and sketches. And the mystery Limoges source of many very useful images.

Mauricette Pinoteau who was so willing to share her knowledge, experience and skill with us and was of invaluable assistance.

James Nowak for three years of help unraveling the mysteries of the Fauré technique.

Bernard Vergne, owner of the Société Allain in Paris, who opened his doors to us and provided extremely valuable information about the forms, spinning and the overall production of the Atelier Fauré.

Paul Buforn, someone else who worked in the Fauré studio and was willing to share information with us.

Michel Kiener (including for some of the photos).

To Eric and Peter from Decodence.

To David Rago and Suzanne Peralaut of the Rago Art Center.

Reid Johnston. Peter Haas. Wolf Eberwein.

The Brohan Collection of Berlin. The Sonnabend Collection: Xan Price and Antonio Homen of New York and Masahiko Shibata of Brain Trust, Tokyo.

Jaci Tomulonus, Monterey Aquarium; Maison Gerard, NYC; Sylvia Tanzer at the Antiquitaeten Zeitung, Germany.

Quittenbaum Kunstauktionen . Louis Meisel. Donna Moreno. Judy Stone.

Tony Fusco for helping me define the direction of this book.

Ahvie and Victoria, for attempting to save the world.

Resources

(Places to look for Fauré)

Shapiro Auctions–Australia

Tajan Auctions–Paris

Sotheby's–Auction rooms about the world

Christie's–Auction rooms about the world

Rago Arts and Auction Center

Decodence Gallery–San Francisco and Florida

Doyle Auctions–New York

info@quittenbaum.de

Treadway-Toomey Auction Gallery–Cinncinatti–Chicago

Mauricette Pinoteau, 6 Blvd Louis Blanc, 87000 Limoges, France, perlesdekaolin@orange.fr

If there is one book you want to read to get a completely comprehensive view of Modernism 1880-1940, it is *Modernism* by Alistair Duncan published by Antique Collectors' Club, without doubt the most comprehensive survey of Modernist design.

Credits

Index

Additional attribution

For reasons of space a few vases for which we do have some information regarding design and execution are included here. It's always interesting with Fauré, where the artists were largely anonymous, to have some information about who they were.

Attributed to M. Bardy. (Private collection, France.)

Attributed to M. Bardy, influenced by A. Marty. (Lucien Geismar collection, France.)

Attributed to M. Rozier. It is worth noting that this piece went on to be made by several other artisans and frequently with poor results. Some of the vases actually look out of focus. The good ones are great and the poor ones shouldn't be bothered with. (Author's collection, San Francisco.)

Attributed to M. Rozier. (Author's collection, San Francisco..)